# New Testament Micro-Ethics

# New Testament Micro-Ethics

On Trusting Freedom: The First Christians'
Genotype for Multicultural Living

by
RAYMOND KEMP ANDERSON

Foreword by Raymond Carr

WIPF & STOCK • Eugene, Oregon

NEW TESTAMENT MICRO-ETHICS
On Trusting Freedom: The First Christians' Genotype for Multicultural Living

Copyright © 2018 Raymond Kemp Anderson. All rights reserved. Except for brief quotations in critical publications or reviews, no part of this book may be reproduced in any manner without prior written permission from the publisher. Write: Permissions, Wipf and Stock Publishers, 199 W. 8th Ave., Suite 3, Eugene, OR 97401.

Wipf & Stock
An Imprint of Wipf and Stock Publishers
199 W. 8th Ave., Suite 3
Eugene, OR 97401

www.wipfandstock.com

PAPERBACK ISBN: 978-1-5326-4738-3
HARDCOVER ISBN: 978-1-5326-4739-0
EBOOK ISBN: 978-1-5326-4740-6

Manufactured in the U.S.A.    10/08/18

All things are yours; and you are Christ's …
    All things are lawful, but not all are helpful.
        All things are lawful, but not all are creative.

—Paul of Tarsus

# CONTENTS

*Foreword by Raymond Carr* | ix
*Preface* | xiii

Introduction: The Minimal Ethic
    of the First Christians' Gospel | 1

1  Jesus' Minimal Ethical Teaching | 3

2  Why a Mustard-Seed Ethic | 15

3  Paul's Cross-Cultural Paraenesis | 23

4  Our Life in Grace Spans Time and Space | 47

5  Paul Urges: Think on These Things | 59

6  In Christ, Be Yourselves | 71

7  Ethics Stripped Down for the World | 79

Abstract | 91

*Bibliography* | 93
*Index* | 97

# FOREWORD
## The Living God and Playful Encounter

*Raymond Carr*

Raymond Kemp Anderson is on to something. He has latched on to (or should I say he has been discovered by) a peculiar wisdom that comes from a special place.[1] To be sure, even from his time as a student of Karl Barth, the grand theologian of the twentieth Century, Anderson has continued to make small contributions and develop his theological vision in an independent direction—a pathway tingling with delight, tiny sparkles of surprise, and the audacity that comes from the truth of one who has witnessed something.[2]

It is my hope that the reader will have ears to hear his witness. For Anderson isolates in this small book the common theme that runs from Jeremiah to Paul, from Augustine to Luther, and from Barth to many others, who have all discovered God's unqualified grace.[3] It is a theme that I hear, parabolically, in black folk traditions fired in the crucible of American experience. Work songs, spirituals, Bessie Smith's blues, and the ironic ludic quality in

---

1. Eph 3:10.

2. See Anderson, *Liberating Speech*.

3. The tradition I am identifying Anderson with is seen in Barth, "Word of God."

## FOREWORD

Thelonious Monk's "Round Midnight" *all* can be heard as witnessing to the fact that "'Life should be play'—not constraint."[4]

Following Anderson, then, these and many others are traditions that can be heard to "incorporate symbols expressive of a Christian community's basic life stance."[5] Of course this is only possible if the church (re)imagines the extraordinary ways the word of God presents itself "outside the walls of the church"—*extra muros ecclesia*—a famous expression of Barth's. If the American church in the mode of discovery opens its eyes and ears to what Anderson has identified as the Sabbatic life, then the church, with God's Spirit accompaniment, can be (re)invigorated and (re)enchanted in light of God's cosmic life-giving vision. Indeed, if it does not happen through inspiration, it will certainly occur more ignominiously; the God of grace is the God of judgment.

The church stands at a threshold moment, but notwithstanding this fact, along with Anderson, I believe the affirmative "yes" of the living God not only shapes our repentance; but God gives shape to the heroic energy of our advocacy, and God calls us into the rhythm of a joyful correspondence between God and humanity. If I might again offer a theological complement to a construction from Anderson's old teacher, Barth, it is my hope that "the God who loves in freedom" will give rise to *a people who freely love!*

For in America—a nation where prosperity has tempted us to hear the "yes" of God in a flat correspondence to human reciprocity (a cheaply misused buzzword)—we fail to honor what it means to live in the joyful rhythms of grace. In such a society, self-righteousness, suspicion, and cynicism take hold. The rhythm of our steps becomes regulated by patriotic songs and military anthems rather than music made for dancing. In such a society, play takes flight!

In short, what I think Anderson is calling us toward in this little book is aimed at encouraging us to laugh, to dance, and to play together again; to engage in a biblical style of life where we

---

4. See Anderson, *On Trusting Freedom*, 80. For the language of "secular spirituals," see Cone, *Spirituals and the Blues*, 102–3.

5. Anderson, *On Trusting Freedom*, 6.

exercise human responsibilities to one another in authentic conversations, improvised communities, and an invocational prayerfulness that truly helps us to discover the richness of the vocational call for all humanity; to even audaciously stumble in a way where the image of the dancing Christ takes the lead and keeps us in the kind of rhythm that emerges out of a playful encounter with God:

> *Jesus, he must dance the lead,*
> *And the Virgin Mary;*
> *All must pay his rhythm heed*
> *To reach God's sanctuary*[6]

---

6. Quoted in Leeuw, *Sacred and Profane Beauty*, 30.

# PREFACE

## THE PERENNIAL SURPRISE

Wriggling into his mother's clothes closet—away from the pursuing voice which sing-songs, "ninety-eight, ninety-nine, one HUN-dred. Here I come, ready or not!"—a small boy suddenly blunders upon a cache of shiny toys hidden away for his coming Christmas. Forgetting all about the game at hand, he stumbles out, stunned, as if given an electric shock. This has been a minor tragedy for him, and he tries to erase from memory his premature glimpse of the hidden gifts. For his is a poor family; and the weeks of anticipation and final delight of discovery are the best part of Christmas, the one great event of the year—a delicious agony of expectation capped by the joy of shared surprise. The worst thing in the world would be to spoil it.

To him it is a strange vice in his red-headed cousin that she prowls about the attic and wardrobes trying to spy out Christmas ahead of time. Her impish grin, as she slips a package's ribbon to peek inside, reminds him uncomfortably of his own urge to pull the wings off butterflies. How could she want to break the spell of carefully kept surprise? Strong feelings, I know—since I was that boy.

It is no accident, as I see it, that sharing small packages of surprise has come to be an important symbol in the main Christian festivals. For the surprise element, a discovery of a goodness which runs counter to virtually all other life experience is central to the Christian faith. The original disciples, who had hoped for a zealous Messiah to make their own nation great again, were surprised by something astoundingly better. And this key experience has not been left behind as an isolated occurrence. It is also there for each new generation and for each new family or community—wherever people discover that belief can be real and that faith may be founded on a singular event with their way of life funded by the claims of Christ.

A people usually will contrive to sound their life's ground tone in the stories and traditions they pass on to their children. It is fitting, then, to preface a book on New Testament life implications by glancing toward the church festivals that have been developed for our children. The St. Nicholas myth, the Easter rabbit, even the Halloween trick-or-treat tradition (which used to have the children of an American town approaching every porch in secure expectancy) all have their element of shared surprise. Despite their banalities and tangled parentage, such folk traditions do incorporate symbols expressive of a Christian community's basic life stance. For they can reflect the surprise and delight of those whose hopes for themselves and for each other have been surpassed at each new insight into God's present grace toward them in Christ. The church is, and is to be, a milieu of expectancy.

The mood of discovery becomes the dominant mode of Christian existence. The spirit of comedy, in the best sense of that word, outflanks the appearance of tragedy. Not only does each new surprise characterize God's ultimate promise for us, it also remains a fresh possibility each day, as often as Christ's claims are remembered with hope.

This surprise, experienced ever new in face of God's unfolding grace, begins to color everything in both the life view and behavior of anyone who has been the least bit attentive to Christ. If we are to be moved towards new styles of action and discover new backing for values and new priorities for decision-making, it will be because our habitual worldview has been transfigured and our action has begun to reflect the extent to which New Testament discoveries have taken us by surprise. If we write or read about Christian life, then we would do well to retain the half smile of those who ever again expect to discover a great deal more in each new relationship than at first meets our eye. Where persons otherwise seem paltry or beyond our reach, unexpected friendship flashes like gold in the pan. Permanent values precipitate from even our most casual or playful moments together.

"Unless you become like little children you will never live into the Kingdom of Heaven," Jesus would say. If childlike surprise and delight at God's goodness are basic to the disciple's life response, there is going to be a special danger for us in talking about Christian life renewal: we may begin to take for granted the subject we are dissecting, to dry up and kill under the microscope a living drama that is to be embraced in constant surprise and wonder. We may risk something of that little girl's violation of Christmas in undertaking research that abstracts and dissects the sources of our life together. Sad to say, our ethics can easily become amoral or even immoral in Christian terms, should we lose the New Testament's own sense of wonder or stifle the spontaneity we are to to enjoy in direct conversation with Christ's living Spirit.

If our approach is to be appropriate to the living reality of our theme in writing (i.e., seeking the mainsprings of the New Testament's thrust in shaping lives), we should show enthusiasm and perhaps even be "burning with spirit," as Paul has it toward the end of his last epistle. Considering the uniqueness of our subject, it would not even be scientifically objective to make cool analysis our main task here. The surprise element of the gospel inspires an attitude of actual expectancy in which life is to be savored to the core as mutual adventure in believed community with the living God.

Dealing with the particular life approach engendered by the New Testament, then, it is imperative that we keep in view the inner spontaneity which is the substance of its person-to-person intercourse and its tenaciously joyful commitments.

At the same time, its implicit mutual respect should keep us from sliding into a merely subjective approach based on sentiment or individualistic feelings alone. Such subjectivity not only would be foreign to the spirit of open investigation, but would undercut respect for each other's insights regarding the God who we may believe became man to give belief a new, objective reference and norm.

Ordinary secular experience has its surprises, too. But it is careless of us as persons and runs towards the ugly. Every day we confront uncontrollable events and imponderable forces which leave us sensing how logical it could be to resign our hopes and adopt a studied apathy. Common experience tends to dictate the common-sense counsel that we mortals should be rational, play it cool, and, like the Stoics, "will in accord with Nature." For nothing to which we may attach ourselves in this world is certain but death, war, and taxes. So don't hope too much of life, and you will not be overtaken by ugly surprises!

But however certain these negative experiences may be, we tend to repress and deny them, and thus adversities tend to take us by surprise. Tax Day bursts in like a bombshell every year; and who is really ready? A lady who happened to be in the room with a number of statesmen when war broke upon their land once told me that none of those "in control" could believe it. The fearful reality took them all by surprise. And again, an undertaker of my acquaintance says he never has entered a house after a death where the event has not struck everyone there as an ugly surprise, even when, rationally speaking, they should have known that it soon must come.

Face up to the certainty of human uncertainty, and the divine constancy of the Christian gospel is all the more surprising. Faith's hope-against-hope possibility always appears like the miracle of a sea anchor where, by riding against the current, it paradoxically draws strength and stability from the very forces that are always most threatening to human life. The gospel is a perennial surprise.

Christ's claims, each time they reappear, float quite free and even run against the tide of ordinary experience. Time after time they flash through the darkness and illuminate the impossibilities of everyman's everyday mortality with new hope and unexpected potential. Our own inconstancy and failure to be even remotely Christ-like heightens by contrast the great surprise claimed for his love.

Hope is the light that cuts through any darkness. A great "Nevertheless!" (always God's possibility) buoys us upwards through our impossibilities. (We may not yet, or may no longer, believe in his love ourselves, but this startling claim stands as an indelible part of our larger human history.) If I even entertain the question of whether God could actually live, the sheer possibility means surprise. Further, if God could be graciously disposed to such as you or me, if the life-giver could be behind Jesus' style of Messiahship, then this possibility heralds good news which is as startling for us today as it ever was. It still means that death itself could be destroyed and all lesser evils with it. Ever and again this very possibility shapes the most hopeful of claims, even for those who find themselves discouraged, or who have been pitched headlong into failure, or who are being overtaken by death itself.

Have you heard? Continual personal surprise belongs to the actual objective history of the faith claims.

Thus, the life of the hearer of any era can become an arena for great expectations. Even in the midst of the worst calamities, we can be refreshed in hope and anticipation. Faith straightens the helm, as it were, against the most discouraging tides of fact. The message which has begun to change everything for all who hear was called "gospel" from the beginning, quite literally meaning astounding "good news."

But this news, by virtue of its otherwise-unknown, yet clearly claimed subject, can never fade into a dead record of the ancient past. This news runs counter to the totality of ordinary experience. The claim persists nevertheless: an all-powerful God lives for good and all—and he lives in such an unexpected and humane way that at each new hearing his message must strike us anew as astounding. From everyday experience, who could have discerned personal meaning behind all that happens? Who could have claimed this gracious compulsion behind the whole universe: God's own compassion to nurture his creatures' freedom and always protect it—even from of any overbearing pressure of his own.

All things considered, this claim strikes us each time we hear it as much too good to be true. Yet for that very reason it remains from day to day, as from age to age, ever again worth proclaiming, always something unexpected, always something new. Though experience declares our faith incredible and foolish, hope fans it into flame.

# INTRODUCTION
## THE MINIMAL ETHIC OF THE FIRST CHRISTIANS' GOSPEL

The great surprise in store for us when we begin to look for the first Christians' ethic or way-of-life teaching may be that there was so little of it.

They called their group "the Way." Yet, when they began to write things down, they had remarkably little to say about how people should live their lives. Specialists have long puzzled over this scarcity of anything like an intentional special ethic in the earliest Christian texts. So, they have worked out various theories to explain why the first believers neglected to detail set instructions for behavior. But for the typical reader who goes to the Gospels seeking rules to apply to thorny everyday issues, this may come as an awkward surprise. A theology student who was cruelly abandoned by her husband tells me of the frustration she felt as she realized how little actual instruction the New Testament gave her on what to do next.

Could it be that Protestants have taken their stand on thin ice, where they have claimed Scripture as their "sole rule for faith and practice"? Must the scarcity of New Testament directives force them either to be content with the Old Testament Law for their ethical footing, or to push out beyond the Scripture-guided life that their confession claims, into the realm of speculation and popular conjecture?

Or could it be that, from the beginning, the gift of Christian faith (even incipient faith; "as small as a mustard seed") always contains within itself a sort of behavioral DNA, a seminal germ for action that, in the light of God's believed presence, will begin to blossom into appropriate action? (See Matt 17:20.) Could it be that Christians' behavior has been left so very unfettered quite purposefully—so it may flow free as a direct personal interchange at each new juncture?

This essay asks whether the earliest Christians were not onto something here: Had they not hit upon a way toward life renewal they found to be at once more authentic and more satisfying than any of the elaborate sets of teachings already available to them? Weren't they taking delight in a new unburdened *Way*, as they called it, flowing out of their faith's attitude of frank, interpersonal conversation? Had they quite consciously discovered a new personal dynamic that was astoundingly liberating, as opposed to the heavy burdens imposed by their ancient tribal traditions and scriptures or by the highly developed moral philosophies of their day? As we shall see, I think it no accident that Jesus was memorialized for just such abandon within the Jewish moral sphere of his day:

> Come to me all who labor and are heavy-laden, and I will give you rest. Take my yoke upon you, and learn from me; for I am gentle and lowly in heart, and you will find rest for your persons. For my yoke is easy and my burden is light. (Matt 11:28)[1]

---

1. Notice further how Matt 11:28–30 fuses this saying to an account of Jesus' shocking use of the traditional Jewish Sabbath rest as safeguard for an unprecedented moral freedom.

# 1

# JESUS' MINIMAL ETHICAL TEACHING

## A SURPRISING SHORTAGE

Contrary to common assumptions, when New Testament scholars summarize the gospel message, they find themselves pointing out that "Jesus teaches no ethics at all"—at least not "in the sense of an intelligible theory valid for all."[1] This observation may take us by surprise. Aren't churches supposed to be teaching people how to behave?

But just listen to some of their negative-sounding reports:

We are reminded by many that it was not a theory of ethics that Jesus taught to the peasants and fisherman who flocked to hear him—"not a colorless abstention from certain vices nor even a performance of a round of stated duties."[2] At least, he did not

---

1. Bultmann, *Jesus and the Word*, 84–85; compare Richardson, *Political Christ*, 71. Bultmann elsewhere speaks of it as typical of early Christian writings that "the ethical paraenesis takes second place" (Bultmann, "Primitive Christian Kerygma," 17).

2. Branscomb, *Message of Jesus*, 103. "It is not . . . identical with any set deeds or habits which we may label as good works. Nor . . . a practical life of

teach ethics in the usual sense of the word. Another reminds us that Jesus was not the author of a code of moral law, or a system of ethics, or of moral theology. The Lord was not crucified for his ethics.[3]

Although this reserve is often overlooked, none of the Gospel writers tries to cast Jesus in the role of a moral teacher.[4] Even the most serious modern scholars often express surprise at how silent is the New Testament about complex social and political life.[5] The themes of political and public life seem to not exist in the New Testament.

These are the voices of respected scholars.

Of course, a contrary view persists on the popular level, and many earnest church people still cling to the nineteenth-century notion that Jesus was predominantly a social reformer. Meanwhile others find textual grounds to take an opposite radical tack and conclude he "had no direct interest in the social problem at all."[6]

On the one hand, some will find grounds to insist that Jesus in word and example delivers a new form of law, a constitution for the Reign of God;[7] On the other hand, some find themselves reflecting that if the teachings of Jesus were indeed intended "as

---

'service'" (Branscomb, *Message of Jesus*, 114); "Jesus was not laying down a hard and fast rule of conduct" (Branscomb, *Message of Jesus*, 121).

3. Reumann, *Jesus in the Church's Gospels*, 223.

4. Matthew may be a possible partial exception, where for a Jewish audience he styles Jesus almost in Moses' shoes. Yet the quality of life perfection described by Matthew, especially in the Sermon on the Mount, lies far beyond the reach of simple human accomplishment; so it functions as much as promise as command to say, "you are to be perfect as God himself is perfect." As we shall see, the life dynamic, described by such perfection-in-command, functions not as a behavioral steroid, but occasions a sense of need and deepens personal dependence upon God, ever-present in Spirit. (Actual new life, then, is a gift experienced through prayerful communion with the Life-Giver, and is not to be claimed as our own accomplishment, virtue, or spiritual growth.)

5. Bultmann, *Primitive Christianity*, 49.

6. Marshall, *Challenge*, 162; Sanders, *Ethics in the New Testament*, 1; Niebuhr, *Interpretation of Christian Ethics*, 51.

7. Klausner: see Manson, *Teaching of Jesus*, 285.

## JESUS' MINIMAL ETHICAL TEACHING

a new law, then something like the rabbinic method of *halakah*[8] would have been appropriate." However, this ethical method, too, is lacking, since the earliest Christian writing goes so far beyond it as to be "quite outside the sphere of law."[9]

Still other scholars are able to assert that Jesus simply depended on Jewish traditions or represented what is universally human and humane; for this reason, there was "no such thing as *Christian ethics*,"[10] since Jesus never said anything that wasn't morally obvious to us. Some even maintain that all the ethical doctrines in the Gospels can be found in previous pagan writers.

What can we conclude from all this? Such contradictory judgments attest to one clear fact: the materials are too sparse to prescribe one's actions. The fact of that scarcity is underlined by the very room the texts leave for wide disagreement, and a wide range of objective thinkers acknowledge that fact. The erstwhile *Honest-to-God* Bishop of Woolwich, John A. T. Robinson, used to declare that the teaching of Jesus, thought of as a moral code, is wholly inadequate."[11] The Göttingen professor, later Bishop of Hanover, Eduard Lohse told us that the notion of a "homogenized" early Christian ethic is "inappropriate."[12] And even so conservative a spirit as New Testament scholar T. W. Manson once observed that "the ethics of Jesus" in the sense of collections of abstract moral precepts and ethical teachings simply "do not exist and have never existed."[13]

So we are left with a strong consensus. In the Christian sources, direct ethical instruction is, to put it mildly, sparse. Yet, this may come as a surprise or even a shock. For it was so long in

---

8. That is, early compilations of the rabbinic rulings which had not been explicit in Mosaic law.

9. Robinson, "Law and Love," 188.

10. Richardson, *Political Christ*, 71–72; Branscomb, *Message of Jesus*, 173.

11. Robinson, "Law and Love," 192. See further Robinson, *Honest to God*, 110–12 for the gist of his view here.

12. Lohse, *Theological Ethics of the New Testament*, 5.

13. Manson, *Teaching of Jesus*, 285; see also Hunter, *Message of the New Testament*, 105.

5

vogue to portray Jesus as a moral pioneer, that people lose track of the fact that such language, if applied to the Gospels at all, could not carry its usual meaning.

A rationalistic nineteenth-century viewpoint that used to be tagged *liberal* left the false impression in many minds that what counted most for the earliest circle of Christians must have been the formation of a "morally religious community based on the teachings of Jesus."[14] It was fateful, Werner Kümmel told us, that F. C. Baur, a key figure in popularizing this speculative approach to Jesus' teachings,[15] "by reason of his presuppositions in the realm of philosophy . . . reduced Jesus' proclamation to a 'purely moral element' and therefore overlooked the significance of Jesus' person in his proclamation."[16] So it is no wonder that there is still a hangover from this view in the popular mind. Meanwhile churches often remain tangled in a painful self-delusion as if their mission would or could be to vaunt their own moral accomplishment as a model.

Even key actors on the theological stage such as Adolph von Harnack (1851–1930) and Albrecht Ritschl (1822–1889) began to take it for granted that a history-bound Jesus must have centered his mission in teaching a simple morality of love or a universal brotherhood, not unlike that of the Stoic philosophers. The theological preoccupations of the Pauline church, as they assumed, are to be regarded as a fall away from the pristine moralism they attributed to Jesus, who "by his teachings sought to lead men to blessedness."

I believe the "liberal" critics, such as F. C. Baur, overlooked a great deal. For beyond the fact we've been noticing, that practical moral teachings are in short supply in the Gospels, it had been grossly distorting for them to trivialize the Apostles' belief in a strong positive relationship between Christ's promise of supranatural future re-creation (eschatology) and present behavior.

---

14. Kümmel, *New Testament*, 142.

15. F. C. Baur (1792–1860), a celebrated rationalistic scholar of Hegelian stamp and founder of the so-called Tübingen School of Biblical Interpretation.

16. Kümmel, *New Testament*, 142.

The gospel tradition organizes all the Jesus material we have around the claims for the revelatory Messiah of *resurrection* belief. His was not essentially the story of an ethical teacher such as nineteenth-century rationalists had begun to project.[17] And even more to the point, as profiles have emerged of certain earlier collections of Jesus materials, which were among the sources of our Gospels,[18] it appears that these too were first assembled in support of the revelatory proclamation of "the resurrection of the one crucified"[19] and intended only very marginally as guidebooks for a pious lifestyle.

The New Testament, as we have it, was formed entirely around the belief in Jesus' transcendent life as revealer of God's own powerful salvation, redemption, and healing intent—not centrally around his ethical teaching. No amount of reading between the lines has been able to pull from the hat, as it were, an original Jesus who was essentially a simple moral pioneer. For as Swiss theologian Emil Brunner once observed, Jesus' scattered moral precepts, such as they may be, refer only to a limited and rather casual assortment of life problems.

The most evidence of the marginalization of ethical teaching in the New Testament may be seen in a rather astounding pronouncement story attributed to Jesus himself. The author of the earliest Gospel, Mark, sets the stage for this at a focal point of his narrative: The crucial question is posed to Jesus by an ethically concerned, potential wealthy donor and benefactor:[20] "What must I *do*" this man asks, to give my life ultimate worth and fulfillment—that is, "to *win* eternal life?"

Jesus disappoints this self-absorbed rich man by telling him to unload his proffered means for self-aggrandizement, divest

17. Bultmann, *Jesus and the Word*; Kümmel, *New Testament*, 337.

18. Most notably, the hypothetical "Q" sayings source collection of Jesus' parables and teachings which was used in both Matthew's revision of Mark and Luke's expanded Gospel alongside other independent sources. See my JSCE study on eschatology and ethics.

19. Kümmel, *New Testament*, 73.

20. See Mark 10. In vv. 22 and 25–26, we have Jesus' unexpected twist regarding self-important "benefactors."

himself of his financial clout, and simply follow. Then when the dumbfounded disciples return to the man's pious-sounding question (What can I do, ethically, to cinch my life's value?), Jesus declares flat-out his shocker: "For people it is impossible!"

You don't hear many sermons on that text: Totally *impossible*! Though seldom regarded, this pronouncement is a cardinal point for Mark: Human worth depends on the attitude and initiatives of God, for whom "all things are possible"[21]—and not on anything I must or even can do.

Though its bald assertion is often ignored, this pericope is placed at a key point in Mark, as it turns toward the gospel's great reversal: the message of the Suffering Servant Messiah. In the perspective of God's grace, that man, as Everyman, was gifted full worth at birth—this quite apart from any legal score sheets or pride the man may be nursing about what he may control. His very question, "What can *I do*?" shows him out of phase with sovereign grace.

The Gospels celebrate an oblique purpose behind Jesus' teachings on unqualified love (even for enemies) as impossible of

---

21. See Mark 10:27. The pronouncement character, as Mark's clear intent for this pericope, is often turned inside out. It has a question posed to Jesus with his sweeping answer. When asked what human action will save us, he makes the shockingly memorable pronouncement that most distinguishes him from the Pharisees: The essential is *impossible* for people to do or earn. It is only possible as God's free initiative. So *follow along* in company with your Savior, who already cherishes you with permanent sovereign intent.

One often meets the assumption that Jesus, like any rabbi, was saying just the opposite—the very antithesis of the point of this pericope, with its focus on human impossibility (as if he were saying, "If you try harder and channel your great wealth more beneficently, that will save you"). Not so!

This chapter acts as the climax of Jesus' teaching ministry in Mark 10. Here his narratives on becoming like children are set in contrast with the zealotistic desire of some of his disciples to make themselves *great*. Then we meet a rich donor who expresses a similar self-centered desire. Jesus' answers with a resounding no way! For people, it is *impossible*! Go *divest yourself* of your special wealth and your claims to superior power and status, and then come and *"follow along,"* Spirit-accompanied, in the train of my freely gifted grace. The unexpected shock of Jesus' pronouncement supports its authenticity.

accomplishment in ordinary human terms.[22] We, the "spiritually impoverished" who languish in humility, "hungry for righteousness" that escapes us, are to be happily blessed.[23]

As Paul attests from Psalms,[24] we all experience this shortfall and find ourselves reaching out for living grace and aid. John Calvin would often characterize the New Testament's paraenesis with his own slogan here: God in his grace asks of us what he knows we in ourselves *cannot* accomplish, "in order that we might grasp what it is we have to ask of him." If God has an everlasting love and sovereign intent to restore us, then this bond of everlasting relationship itself is the key concern.[25]

Through many years of teaching Christian ethics I've come to realize that contrary to popular assumptions, the New Testament, taken as a whole, lacks a fleshed-out program. But we still need to face up to the question of what it meant if this lack was no accident: What if it was quite intentional on the part of the apostolic writers? What if, while happily urging a whole new approach to behavior based on living memories of Jesus and his clash with the Pharisees, they took purposeful care to avoid imposing a set of canons for behavior?

In this study we ask if the omission of such directives clearly reflects the first Christians' conscious, revolutionary change of attitude. Was a pointedly liberated approach to action expressive of the new life stance these people so enthusiastically embraced? Could it be that as a people, they found themselves so affected in

22. Here I think of Eduard Thurneysen's description from a Swiss mountain climber's perspective: "The Sermon on the Mount's take on life confronts us like a sheer cliff, lacking handholds and towering an *impossible* thousand meters above. The call to mount it throws us back into a prayerful dependence on God, as he is known in Christ, to lift us with his forgiveness and renewal" (my translation and emphasis; see also the English translation of this remarkable text, *Die Bergpredigt, Theologische Existenz Heute*, as Thurneyson, *Sermon on the Mount*). See my Barth retrospective (*American Scholar*, 315–16).

23. Matt 5:3–6.

24. Rom 3:10–24; 11:32; Gal 3:22; Ps 14:1.

25. Consider Rom 12:32. Compare Løgstrup (*Ethical Demand*, 111), who from a slightly different angle spoke of the same *impossibility* in Christian ethics. See also Moltmann, *Ethics of Hope*, 122.

their direct person response that they began to slough off external judgmental criteria and behavioral formulae as superfluous burdens? Didn't they, as Christ's followers, take quite conscious delight in declaring themselves truly liberated here? We know many had come to believe that the prophet Jeremiah's promise was being fulfilled in their own corporate life "in Christ":

> Behold, the days are coming, says the LORD, when I will make a new covenant . . . I will put my law within them, and I will write it upon their hearts . . . And no longer shall each one teach his neighbor . . . for they shall all know me, from the least of them to the greatest. . . . (Jer 31:31–34)

It must have been the fulfillment of this promise that the principal Christian thinker, Paul of Tarsus, had in mind when he told the Corinthians with such abandon that in his response to Christ, "all things are lawful!"[26] It is but a further expression of the same sense of liberation that lets Paul, in the next breath, trust his own discernment regarding which possible actions would not be "useful."

That is, he seems to be claiming that we, like him, are free to discover for ourselves the behavior that would be appropriate to uphold and express our community in Christ. So he explains that although all things are lawful, not all things "build up" the covenant relationship we enjoy in free response to Christ.[27]

For to be a Christian, as someone has remarked, "is at root to share that style of relationship with God which Jesus initiated."[28] The ethical question then becomes what are the implications of that living relationship in the here and now.

In exploring these things, I would hope to explode one of the most common popular stereotypes today: the notion that our faith is of a mind to dictate set patterns for behavior, and enforce its authority with threats of punishment and promises of

---

26. 1 Cor 10:23; 9:20–21.
27. 1 Cor 10:23.
28. Houlden, *Ethics and the New Testament*, 17 and 125.

reward—sometimes by claiming a hold over God's (or Allah's) final judgment pictured as paradise or hellfire.[29]

Nothing, I fear, could be further from the motivational power of Christians' healing message than this caricature. And sad to say, nothing is more repellent to us wayward and lost human beings for whom the church exists, given its Christic mission as leaven, salt, and light for our Godless (and god-obsessed) world. Not even the ancient prophets, with their florid warnings regarding the direct consequences of community-destructive practices, were that wooden. For they knew the very womb of all life is God's creative *chesed*—his staunch initiative as loyal love.

Our prolific theological writer, Stanley Hauerwas, did well to chime in with Mennonite ethicist John Howard Yoder on this point: Christians' "moral judgments are not deductive applications of universally valid rules, but the confrontation of one person by another on matters that matter for the whole community."[30] Though, one may wonder at how Hauerwas, perhaps predestined by his Methodist roots, can take it so for granted that we are equipped to "change the way things are by changing ourselves." I can't help but question whether by cheer-leading for habitual virtues[31] we can actually determine who people become in their innermost selves. Isn't moral, as well as physical stature in question when Jesus asks, "Who, by taking thought, can add a cubit to his stature?" (Matt 6:27; Luke 12:25–26.)

Our spontaneous response to God's love in Christ is, and is to be, a far cry from a self-imposed program of duties or virtues.

---

29. Such views become prominent in medieval views (as also in the Qur'an), which go back to an OT understanding of God's justice as retributive equity, apart from Jesus' redefinition of a contributory justice and the creedal claim that the Christ, the Healer, will be our only final judge.

30. Hauerwas, *Christian Existence Today*, 73.

31. Hauerwas, *Christian Existence Today*, 74.

## LIFE IN CHRIST—NO MERE DUTY

It was pounded into me from childhood that no matter how we felt, we must do our "Christian duty." So it came as a surprise to me when the personalist moral philosopher John Macmurray, at the University of Edinburgh, pointed out to us that Jesus Christ is remembered to have mentioned *duty* only a single time. And then with but a negative, dismissive shrug: They are "unworthy servants" who have only "done what was their *duty*" (Luke 17: 10).

Across the entire New Testament we discover that we are, and are to be, completely free, whole-hearted, and willing in our response to God's grace in Christ. Any forced belief or grudging action is sub-Christian and falls far short of the full inner freedom of love's response. This means that the very notion of *Christian duty*, at least as we Californians had understood it, is practically speaking an oxymoron, a contradiction of terms.

A friend was puzzling how he might answer another acquaintance who had almost sneered that the gospel claims are simply not *compelling*. My friend didn't yet appreciate how in our Christian perspective such an observation is quite true and extremely important. Indeed, we need to reflect on what it means if the greatest power of the universe has in fact carefully avoided ever *compelling* us. For we are blessed with the unavoidable yet non-provable claim that the loving Lord bends over backwards (and cross-wards) to leave us, his beloved creatures, *free of compulsion*—even as he, all the while, does everything to win our whole-hearted relationship. The Gospels are careful to record that our Lord, though representing Ultimate Power, always left room for those around him to question, doubt, or even deny him. That was essential for faith's freedom and must always remain background for the gospel claim.

The Gospels of Mark and Luke describe God's representative Messiah as beginning his appeal to man by rejecting, once and for all, as satanic any temptation to take people over by force, whether by force of arms, by tyrannical divine control, or by *compelling* mental assent through some miraculous proof. (See Matt 4 and Luke 4.) Surprisingly suggestive events burst out around Jesus.

Yet when he is asked to repeat some striking deed for miraculous proof, he refuses: No such sign will be given (Luke 11:29).

It is an essential grace and kindness that faith is never forced upon us. So whenever we mistakenly refer to *faith* as compelling *knowledge*, it falls short and actually becomes a sub-Christian expression. Yet being human and fallible, we of the church have again and again had bad moments when we've vainly tried to bolster faith with tyrannical authority, towering buildings, high-flown argument, or awe-inspiring spirituality—all a sad departure from the simple claim that God's attitude is revealed in Christ's grace and that his Spirit inspires our action in wide-open community—not as duty, but freely as sheer gift.

# 2

# WHY A MUSTARD-SEED ETHIC

We are suggesting that the earliest Christians may well have treasured their new life *in Christ* as a form of liberation, which they saw as the longed-for fulfillment of Jeremiah's prophecy. The long-heralded day of the Lord has come when the Jewish people's liberating covenant life would well up spontaneously as a direct response[1]—a heartfelt living intercourse with the self-revealing Lord.

But in mentioning *spontaneity* in this connection, there is an immediate danger that this term may be shackled by a habitual mentality and indentured to serve as its very opposite: reduced to a compelling duty or prescribed set of virtues.

I have in front of me a "Born Loser" cartoon. That bumbling man stands at his morning bus stop mumbling that his wife has told him he needs to be more "off the cuff." So rehearsing her advice, he mutters, "From now on I'll have strict guidelines I'm going to follow to be more *spontaneous*."[2]

---

1. Jer 31:31. Cf. Heb 8:10.

2. There is danger of a fundamental misunderstanding of the gift of spontaneity, as if this gift were a virtue to be preached as part of a dutiful program for proud achievement through human grit and gumption, rather than a simple intuitive interaction. For a poignant parallel, see Charles Dickens's portrayal in *David Copperfield* of Uriah Heep's oily obsequiousness in boasting

## A WORLD-SPANNING LIFE PERSPECTIVE

It may be worth noting here that it was in the nineteenth century's climate of evolutionary "optimism" that Jesus was re-styled as having been essentially an *ethical pioneer* who pushed a humanistic program for mankind's virtuous moral development. That era's enthusiasm for a closed universe, whereby the totality of reality was thought to be accessible to man's empirical knowledge, must strike us as rather naive and obsolete today. For scientists, especially physicists, have become aware of a host of realities that stretch far beyond our empirical tools to grasp them. The narrowly positivist "optimism" is now recognized by scientists as having settled into an unwarranted narrow speculation. In its drive to escape idle superstition, a rather puerile natural science had felt pushed to ignore and abandon our greatest human potential—an openness toward the incalculable Unknown and Unseen. It had become tone-deaf to the virtually infinite possibilities which lie beyond human means to measure or fully comprehend.

Those who, like F. C. Baur, had given up on possibilities beyond materialistic human control, had been embarrassed by the Bible's supernatural reference. So feeling constrained to shrink their hopes to an anthropometric scale, they became agile at side-stepping the Apostolic church's openness to the Unseen and its hopes for supra-human promise and freedom. They tended to assume that since Jesus was in some sense a source for Western

---

another so-called Christian virtue of *humility*. Such arrogance was foresworn in the early church as self-deceptive pharisaism (see Eph 2:8).

We shall see how this has its analogue in a tragic misconception of even the most basic "theological virtues" (faith, hope, and love). A twisted Pharisaic attitude toward these gifts of grace vaunts them, as if these "fruit of the Spirit" were superior human achievements or as if true *obedience* could be forced upon anyone. In Christian theology, the concept of obedience itself denotes a whole-hearted attunement to another person, which is from first to last a gift when you discover it in yourself. (See Anderson, *American Scholar*, 108–20.)

The Reformers, as defenders of Christians' freedom, found that popular notions of *free will* were often so blind to this deeper dimension as to render them practically unusable (see Luther's debates with Erasmus, "On the Freedom of a Christian" and Calvin's *Institutes* [II.ii.7–8]).

culture,[3] he must have been pushing a plan for practical behavior, whereby people could bolster their own self-fulfillment and well-being.

Never mind that such a narrowing of focus to the sphere of human powers (or virtues) was totally foreign to the Reformation's rediscoveries in New Testament faith. The assumption was simply carried forward that the supra-human enthusiasms of the first Christians must have been marginal to Jesus' humanistic significance and so, dispensable.

When Albert Schweitzer[4] and New Testament scholar Johannes Weiss finally threw over the "liberal" assumption that Jesus must have centered his mission in promoting a humanistic ethic, they based their objections largely on textual and technical grounds. Schweitzer, having faced up to the evidence that the Jesus materials showed a strongly eschatological orientation,[5] went to an opposite extreme to interpret Jesus, not as a moral pioneer, but as an apocalyptic enthusiast.[6] So Schweitzer now stressed that the

---

3. Some would try to explain Jesus as a function of historical process or historical synthesis in the Hegelian sense. I draw attention here to scholarly trends as one source of interpretations that have gradually been popularized and become widely influential. Yet one should bear in mind that most grassroots congregations and perhaps even a majority of academic theologians never really bought into such anti-supernatural rationalisms. Meanwhile, some of the most incisive philosophical writers, most notably Søren Kierkegaard, never lost objective openness to the Unknown or the transcendent possibilities of faith.

4. Schweitzer, a musical genius and Bach interpreter, wrote a game-changing critique of all the contradictory popular attempts to reconstruct a historical Jesus, and in his later years he received *Time* and *Life* magazine fame as the white-helmeted missionary doctor of Lambaréné, who preached a simplified doctrine of reverence for life.

5. Schweitzer made a slogan of his *"consequent eschatology"* recognizing Jesus' deep concern for "last things" (i.e., expectations regarding life's supernatural end-goal, resurrection, afterlife, etc.).

6. Apocalyptic beliefs anticipated a final unveiling or inbreak of God's overwhelming power and spawned colorful images of the cataclysmic events whereby he will finally crush out all evil.

Lord shared primitive belief in an impending supernatural inbreak and end of the world.[7]

According to Schweitzer's presuppositions Jesus must have expected the end to follow directly upon his ministry. Accordingly, Schweitzer assumed this eschatology would have made the earliest Christians lose interest for life in the world (which, as they came to believe, was soon to be cut short). But he supposed that, as post-resurrection life later dragged on for them with no end in sight, they would have been forced to improvise appropriate patterns for continuing life together in human society. So, in his view, the church itself must have begun to patch together some kind of *interim ethic,* where at first such ethical teaching would have seemed superfluous.[8]

For those who, like Schweitzer, were wedded to a rather dualistic nineteenth-century metaphysics, it became almost inevitable to assume that the first Christians' focus on super-naturalistic beliefs about an imminent end of the age must have made any planning for behavior in this material world seem unnecessary and dispensable in the earliest church.

Indeed, the apocalyptic transcendent reference of Jesus' own life and teaching appears beyond question today. But it also should have become clear to us that Jesus' apocalyptic had little or nothing in common with the dualistic eschatologies which were ubiquitous in the conflicted cities of the Hellenist world, where world-abandonment and speculative "knowledge" (*gnosis*) claiming various esoteric pathways for the human spirits' escape from physical

---

7. Compare Moltmann, *Way of Jesus Christ,* 316.

8. We may notice here that Rudolf Bultmann's later program for the church to "demythologize" its use of New Testament literature was little more than a correlate to this, Schweitzer's view, applied to other sectors with the closed physical universe (itself a peculiarly nineteenth-century mythology) taken for granted. Probably no other event will turn out to have been more fateful, or problematic, in the field of theological ethics during the last century than the metaphysical self-assertiveness with which Bultmann displaced the Reformation's location of Christians' new life in God's decisive action in grace (i.e., in "God's own sovereign election"), to think of it instead as centered in our own existential decision (see Cullmann, Études *de Theologie Biblique,* 132–43; see also Cullmann, *Christ and Time,* 231–42).

## WHY A MUSTARD-SEED ETHIC

entanglements were commonly embraced as the stuff of salvation. Indeed these were frequently fused onto the gospel message.

Close study of the Judaic eschatology, however, does not support Schweitzer's presupposition that the Jews of Jesus' day expected such a radical disjunction between the present eon and the age to come.[9] It is simply incorrect to suppose Jesus and the people around him would share the notion—still abroad today—that hope for future life could apply only to the *spiritual* dimension of ourselves. The Bible has no concept of a built-in soul, possessed of deathless immortality that will slough off bodily identity like a cocooned butterfly at death.[10] (As if the human wholeness we have known in our dramatic intercourse as embodied persons, with unique histories, were unworthy of a future.) When Paul spoke of resurrected or, better, re-created *"spiritual bodies"* (a term that would have sounded like an oxymoron in Hellenistic ears), he was not thinking of a total break between our present bodily experience and our future. For he believed the whole historic named personality can be re-created and restored somehow by God's grace.

So although Schweitzer's recognition of New Testament eschatology was correct, the assumptions he made, spiritualizing it, were anachronistic. For they were skewed by Western philosophical notions which assumed that the time-space dimensions of creaturely relationships must end for us along with our life in this physical world. (As Schweitzer saw it, that would mean justice between us in the here and now would have little or no future analog; so, as he supposed, those excited in their expectation that the end

---

9. See Wright, *Surprised by Hope*, 111–13. Wright is rightly scandalized by wrong-headed world-escape theologies that still, today, with their heaven and hell imagery, ignore the gospel's deep concern for present life in the material world. Wright is so scandalized, I fear, that he may neglect the further transcendent, afterlife dimensions of gospel promises, such as John 14:2–3. Revolutionary re-creation beliefs also had breath-taking supra-cosmic dimensions, such as those essential for Paul (as in 1 Cor 15). These remain more vital for Christians' hope in the face of death than the concomitant restoration of this world that so preoccupies Wright. (Compare *Revolution*, 67–69, and throughout.)

10. See Cullmann, "Immortality of the Soul."

was soon to come would have given short shrift to ethical concerns about shaping life in this physical world.)

Such dualistic notions, virtually axiomatic in the Hellenistic world, made fateful incursions into the field of Christian ethics and are shared by many to this day.[11] I suspect further investigation of the Schweitzer-Weiss hypothesis will reveal that such presuppositions resulted from intrusions of European metaphysics that obscured Jesus' view of the transcendent, already present and yet still-to-come eternal Reign of God. If, as the Bible has it, Time and Place are themselves entirely God's good creation, then he has been free to engender a plenitude of times and spaces eternally place marked for his creatures in their wholeness.[12] And as Creator of Time itself, wouldn't he have something like a simultaneous embrace of all our times as a whole, if we are truly his beloved creation? As we shall see, St. Paul seems to have envisioned God's holistic grasp of our lives in such terms.

## THE JUDAIC FOCUS

The growing Judaic eschatological enthusiasm of Jesus' day was focused on God's community-restorative action to fulfill the holistic Creation he had embraced as good from the very beginning.[13] Afterlife was to bring no complete break with his people's earthly story which always had been embraced by his liberating intent. (Even the laws of Moses were believed to support the Exodus community's liberated life in sabbatic interdependence.)[14] There

11. See e.g., Sanders, *Ethics in the New Testament*, 29.
12. Compare Wright, *Surprised by Hope*, 109–22, especially 115.
13. Gen 1:31.
14. Space is lacking here to show how a sabbatic stance toward all of life issued in what could well be termed a *sabbatic ethic*. For life resting in full dependence on the Liberator God and embodied in his liberty-upholding covenant was fundamental to the Mosaic desert saga and to Judaic ethic and law. (This sabbatic life attitude found reinforcement in the post exilic priestly creation saga [Gen 1] that symbolically bracketed the entire world's creation with God's seven day Sabbath provision.) Elsewhere I would show how *life-at-rest*—resting in full dependence on the Liberator God's initiatives and

## WHY A MUSTARD-SEED ETHIC

was no myth of a deathless human spirit flitting away from the grosser physical side of life. Any resurrection was to be holistic and include something analogous to a bodily dimension in a restored corporate life.

There is no reason, then, to suppose that the eschatology which Christ fused into that of many other Jews of his day was any less expectant of a whole-life covenant renewal. Such life renewal in the emergent Judaic sense meant the very opposite of an end to their mutually responsive, interdependent life together.[15] Any future re-creation—a perfection of our finest inter-personal existence—would include a plenitude of human-scaled restored Time and Place. Since it is to be essentially a matter of whole person engagement, our future restored life may have its beginnings—the full-bodied first fruits of Holy Spirit accompaniment— here and now. So there could be no thought of an only temporary *interim ethic* in Schweitzer's terms.

Our literature in the area of eschatology, however, is still larded with a bunch of concepts foreign and counter to Judaic beliefs.[16] Should such inappropriate language still color our preconceptions, it may be difficult to avoid the fate of those who, along with Schweitzer, remain blind to some of the most characteristic dimensions of emerging Judaic eschatology—especially its creation-

---

embodied in and emboldened by his liberty-upholding covenant—was utterly fundamental to Judaic ethic and law. Hence, it is to be understood not only that Judaic ethic was a sabbatic ethic, but that the way of Christianity always shared this quality. Compare Moltmann on "The Messianic Sabbath" and the life it evokes (119–21).

15. For survey accounts of the Judaic material in question see Hans Schubert, *Die Religion*, 34–68; and Sigal, *Emergence of Contemporary Judaism*. Conservatives, such as the Sadducees, considered such afterlife hopes (though popular in the synagogues) unwarranted by the Scriptures.

16. The term "eschaton" itself, referring to "last things," is already slanted toward dualism; whereas, in the emerging afterlife hopes of first-century Judaism, the end of earthly life was only in the most penultimate way believed to be the end of YHWH's full story with us. Other alien notions include a state of disembodied spiritual or timeless existence, the end of time, our absorption like water droplets in a vast spiritual sea, etc. See Wright, *Surprised by Hope*, 154–59, 35–37.

bound, human-scaled, and even materialistic aspects. If, given our background, we notice these at all, we may still tend to neuter our Creed's more vivid expectations regarding a person-dimensioned *resurrection of the body* before God, and demote them to the status of "symbolic-mythological" or, even more condescendingly, primitive anthropomorphic expressions.

# 3

# PAUL'S CROSS-CULTURAL PARAENESIS

## THE DYNAMICS OF FREE COMMUNION

The writings of Paul of Tarsus are the earliest complete documents we have from the emerging Christian church. From textual studies I am convinced that the intent to keep ethical teaching in a most simple, seminal form was important to Paul's gospel message. This is true even of his earliest letter.[1] There is also evidence that this was already a treasured quality of the good news for the very first Christians before him. Wherever we can ferret out strands of their thinking imbedded in our New Testament, this seems to have been the case. Apparently, their gospel already evoked a flexible, stripped-down approach to life formation which they felt to be liberating. This attitude has reverberated in great theologians' teaching on the moral life. Think of Augustine's famous dictum: "Love God; and then loving him, do as you please!"

1. That is, almost certainly, 1 Thessalonians. Galatians has sometimes been thought to be Paul's earliest letter, but for a number of reasons, this is not likely, especially given its close textual proximity to his crowning summation, Romans.

And then, above all, think of the Reformers' revolt against medieval concepts of score sheet merit and elaborate canon law which they found poisonous to believers' confidence.

Certainly not all the early Christians stressed the same things or agreed in detail, though they all centered their grasp of *the new Way* in memories of Jesus.[2] So it is overly simplistic to speak of the Early Christians' *kerygma* in a formulaic way, as some have done. But as said, even in those places in the New Testament where bits of their earliest proclamations can be identified,[3] it is evident that this attitude was important to them from first: The motivational springs for a new practical life are gifted, So the expression of one's life in Christ, quite purposefully, should be left open-ended and free.[4]

All creatures are to be recognized for what they are already and are to be permanently in God's unqualified grace. They are to be respected as already one with each other in Christ's freedom-tending love, and their life is to be lived with that in view. That is, each person is called to be freely herself *on that basis*—to become who she finds herself finally to be in *that* reoriented perspective—and so, to trust her own and others' creative self-expressions as direct responses to Christ's embrace.[5]

---

2. See Karl Barth's comment on pages 49-50 below, footnote 3.

3. Most notably, there are two passages in Paul where he explicitly identifies teachings that "had been traditioned" (παρέδωκα) to him as of primary import when he first became a Christian. (See 1 Cor 11:23–5 and 15:3–5.) Further, there are a number of other identifiable instances of the earliest creedal summaries, hymns, slogans, titles for Jesus, and common OT proof texts or *homologia*—all apparently clues to certain widely shared kerygmatic patterns. So, though space is lacking to demonstrate all this here, I feel justified in speaking in broad terms of early kerygmatic key beliefs which are still in sharp focus in the later writings of Paul.

4. Although written to speak to the popular movements of the 1960s, Baker's *Open End* does show how purposeful was this essential attitude.

5. *Metanoio*, discovering a reorientation of mind, is the operative word for Paul. (As we've mentioned, it is usually quite inadequately translated as *repent*.). Paul often comes to speak of our being "thus-minded" or having "the mind of Christ" in us. (See, e.g., Phil 2:5–8; 3:15; Rom 8:6–27; 12:2; 1 Cor 2:16.) See further page 62, footnote 11 and p. 82, f.n. 4.

This means that essentials for appropriate action (that ethicists are in the habit of dissecting into separate factors) are *given* to us already as part of faith's discovery in and through the Christ events: Our actual life *situation* is constantly revised by faith in the unseen One, whom Christ represents; our only *norm* for behavior is his freely responsive love; our *warrant* for action is God's own life-giving covenant; our *motivation* is his response-winning grace; and our *backing* is his promise, mediated by Christ and taken up by countless witnesses. His ways are not our ways; yet all these dimensions are given to us through the incarnate Word, who from the beginning has buffered them with meticulous care in order to leave us free. None of these things is our own achievement, yet they begin to slide into priority as we act in company with him; and we find ourselves gratefully oriented by them.

Here we can begin to know ourselves, as we truly are known.[6] There is no other *me*, finally, who can subsist other than as this covenanted self. Here I am to find and be myself with confidence. For we are loved by the One who frees and empowers us to discover and accept ourselves in a gifted togetherness of the widest order.

## PERSON RESPONSE: UNIQUE AND DIVERSE

Turning back to Paul to ask what becomes of the seminal ethic from Jesus in the life of the emerging churches, we have to bear in mind that the Apostle was notorious among his peers for the practical freedom he found bolstered by Christ within the Jewish ethical tradition. For Paul was radical in his insistence that free relational response to Christ's accompanying Spirit is to supersede any compelling prescriptive norms in the actual formation of Christians' behavior. He was severely denounced for just that by some Jerusalem Christians. He was confident that those within a Christ-aware covenanted community will find themselves gradually drawn toward solidarity with "the many,"[7] all of whom God

6. See 1 Cor 13:12 and context.

7. N.B., this NT term for the beneficiaries of Christ echoes an Aramaic idiom for *general public* (i.e., *hoi polloi*, "the many" = *all* people) without

loves. That would be just as inevitable as breathing out follows breathing in.

It is suggestive here that the ancient words for Spirit are closely related to breath stream metaphors.[8] Once the Holy Spirit has in-*spir*ed us, that inspiration will quite simply be breathed out again—expressed outwardly to others. Yet the response of the next person, in turn, is and is to be a fresh Spirit-inspired event (uniquely her own), the expression and product of her own encounter.[9] And this serves to create a glorious wealth of diversity within the larger community of our corporate body.

Each personal interaction, then, is of a particular moment, and each moment's action can have eternal worth for God, affirmed and preserved as such by his awesome power to clasp and conserve the richly diverse whole of our life as priceless and irreplaceable.

There is no ground here for our society's tendency to treat people like replaceable cogs or mere "human resources" in the production machine. Within God's grace we are all ends in ourselves and are to be respected and valued as such—all to find place in his everlasting corporate embrace.

The worth and dignity that this perspective wins for our singular moments can be an antidote to the cynical indifference toward the mere individual that infects most socialistic endeavors. For God upholds the full worth of each person here and now as the irreplaceable tissue of our covenanted wholeness. Since that unity harbors an unending wealth of diversity, each individual in reach of any organization is to be regarded as an equally important stakeholder.

---

further qualification. (See for example Rom 5:15, 19 and 12:5: 1 Cor 10:17.). Significantly, the formula for the Eucharist may have had this idiom behind it: Christ's blood "poured out for [*the*] *many*"; i.e., for *all* (Mark 14;24; Matt 26:28).

8. Greek: *pneuma* and Hebrew: *ruah, nephesh*. Compare Jesus' interchange with Nicodemus (John 3:1–8): the *wind/spirit* (*pneuma*) blows/*inspires* (*pnei*) where it will (i.e., in complete freedom).

9. Recall Emil Brunner's observation that truth itself, for us, becomes a matter of encounter (*Divine-Human Encounter*, 7).

It is important to bear in mind that love is always personal, definite, and concrete—always of the One who is for one and of each for others, for all; always an event between actual persons who have their own stories and bear their own names. As such, love is an essential and irreducible substance of their irreplaceable histories. And the claim is that these are to be upheld by God's abiding power to affirm, forgive, accept, and restore. Love, then, must be opportunistic (here in a very special and beautiful sense) for it can be received only as the potential of actual relationship in time and place. It is a function of lived moments with all the givenness of their circumstance, all their kaleidoscopic peculiarity, intact.

I once said to my brother, a pioneer heart surgeon, "Let's not complicate things." Typical of his experience, he replied, "But isn't that what life is—a series of complications?" Love always opens to the real complications of the moment and affirms each moment as unique, just as the persons involved are unique. So love will be imaginative to live in explicit newness and treasure the moment. Thus our lives participate in God's ongoing creation, being always something new of everlasting worth. There will be flowers to pluck and give away at each new turning in the garden of circumstance. Authentic and appropriate expressions are never frozen down for all times and places, but are to be gathered from the near at hand, among the opportunities that present themselves in the givenness of each life situation. Love empowers imaginative interplay using the materials at hand for fresh expression.

A young couple strolls through a mountain glade . . . A blue glint of gentian catches the eye. The man stoops, picks, and hands his companion a dew-sweet flower. She binds it in her hair. No word is spoken, yet the meaning may never be forgotten. And as they continue, they are walking hand in hand.

Yes, love is and should be opportunistic, always drawing its best expressions from the simple materials at hand, such as the "cup of cold water" offered in character with Christ.[10] The opportunities are endless: from dish washing or hedge clipping, on one

---

10. Mark 9:41; Matt 10:42.

hand, to the delight of nestled nakedness, on the other; where even our sexual drive may be either pledged and shared with passionate abandon, or held at bay with tendered continence in keeping with prior family bonds and commitments.

But there are the limiting cases, too, where crooked circumstances are so twisted by evil and death that love's immediate options are almost beyond recognition. Yet even in a bloody battle, love can draw life from the brute materials at hand. Love may be most itself when in a last split second, in order to shield others, you pull a trigger or leap on a live grenade. Just so, love shapes its most appropriate expressions from our living drama here and now—including the spontaneous opportunism of the crosses we bear: "Greater love hath no man than this."

And though an outer similarity between past and present situations may tempt us to categorize past decisions and lump them together under a blunt casuistry, creative interplay is to remain a touchstone for Christians' action. For Jesus would speak of our being the spice of others' life: fresh—*salty* with our wit and buoyant with good humor, like *yeast*, bringing levity and light-heartedness into every situation. To be Christ-like, then, is not to mimic Jesus' first-century moves, but to be breathing in his freedom and responding directly to him now in contemporary ways with modern means. So making a real goulash of Jesus' own mix of metaphors, we can say the unique life expressions of our here and now are to glow, a luminous part of his precious whole. Each fresh moment is to be skeined into the there-and-then immediacy of God's own permanent knowledge of us—to take its place in the many-mansioned covenant life that is our corrosion-resistant, moth-proof, permanently secure treasure in heaven."[11] (This itself could be thought of as an alternative cosmos, somewhat analogous to, but distinct from our own or perhaps as his own perfect grasp of our entire story objectified somehow for us to enjoy. Who knows?)

There is a further implication of our freedom response, however, which may not be immediately apparent. Within this perspective, God remains free to affirm our moments, even when we

11. Matt 6:19–20.

remain, as my students would have put it, tight-assed—when we quite freely let ourselves slide along in a defensive adherence to virtue-tagged habits or commit to disciplines that another person in another time and place might find quite contrary to her own freedom in grace.[12]

But a person following Christ does not abandon the world to keep herself unsullied and special. And neither will she be careless of her awesome freedom and let it slide into a careless libertinism.[13]

The same may be said for any social patterns and mores we may find useful in order to become "incarnate" in a particular culture and thus better communicate there. (See Chapter 5.) "When in Rome do as the Romans do."[14] But you don't thereby set one culture above the other. Paul, in claiming such freedom does not thereby imply that other Jews must leave their purification rites in order to be true Christians, nor that all Greeks who would share the Jewish Messiah's hope must first be circumcised, or that in order to be free in Christ all slaves must first manage manumission (though the Apostles did enjoin and welcome their promised liberation). For the very moment any rule of discipline becomes prescriptive and apodictic (as if it were to be a precondition for personal worth, Christian existence, or salvation), it has been torn from the arena of grace-responsive freedom and has become, in effect, an idol leaning away from God's liberating intent.

The exact content of our response to the living Spirit in life, then, is not prescribed, not pre-scripted, but free to be flexible—just

---

12. Paul, on occasion, speaks positively of self-disciplines that we may freely adopt, to train our bodies or to learn skills. Such was the tough apprenticeship he must have endured to master his tent manufacture or the practice to which I must commit if I am to play a trombone or become a surgeon.

We are to do such things as an expression of full *freedom in Christ*, but not at its expense. Just so, I may not put the regimen I am following or the rigors of my particular discipline between myself and anyone else, or give my behavior the appearance of being necessary to our full worth before God. Thus, self-discipline on occasion may be a liberated activity.

13. 1 Cor 5:9–11.

14. This saying, though wrongly attributed to Paul, does express the responsive flexibility of his ethics. Compare Gal 2:11–13; 4:12; 1 Cor 9:19–23.

as subtle and complex as is our past history and all the other variables touching our moment.

But here we'll want to make sure that another common misunderstanding is put to rest. Flexibility within our life context does not mean sloppy imprecision, as one might suppose at first glance, but quite the opposite: We are free to seek *the one best way* that is most clearly our own response to the freedom-bestowing God in Christ, as he is believed present to our situation, just here, just now. Resilient adaptability does not mean all-permissive flaccidity and carelessness. Rather, freedom in Christ occasions careful exactitude: making your scalpel cuts fit whatever abscess you're lancing, making your words respond to just this person's feelings.

Again, responsive freedom here means just the opposite from the moral defeatism which is satisfied that "anything goes," or that my puny existential decisions determine all that goodness can mean for me.

As one becomes attentive to the sovereign and living grace of the universal Creator, each moment begins to reverberate with yearning for guidance, a prayerful attitude. Not even the hallowed tablets of law, which describe in generalities a covenanted freedom, are precise enough to predetermine our appropriate response in this one-and-only here and now. There are at each point in time particular ways of acting that best express *who you are* for him. One course of action can be expressly *yours*, your own response to the fact of who he is and who these others, your everlasting friends, are.

Paradoxically, perhaps, at some moments this can mean you do accept an insouciant and indeterminate dice toss as *the way* at a moment when all else seems equal or the alternatives obscure.[15] But even when we feel ready to shoot in the dark or hazard ourselves, this too can be a definite confident way before him.

So there is an unqualified directness, a more than custom-built uniqueness of ethical imperative, to shape our involvement in every event. We are called to live with eyes and ears wide open,

---

15. The Reformers spoke often of recognizing *adiaphora*, where outer form is of little consequence.

attentive to his incarnate love. We experience ourselves as being concurrently attuned to the Word with the expectant, attentive *hearing* denoted by the biblical concept *obedience*. So what we are describing is a higher level of more explicit, more personal obedience (in the biblical sense of that word) than any program of case- or canon-law can engender.[16]

In fact the temptation to retreat into formal prescriptions for behavior may be an ego-defensive strategy. Not trusting ourselves or others, we may be hiding from direct person-engagement behind pre-scripted mechanical moves.

So every legalistic attempt to tack down "*the Christian* ethic" or "*the Christian* virtues" may sin against the Spirit, for it risks obscuring the integral, living value of each moment's action as a unique event in the living story of God's community. Where the drama of salvation is concerned, one unwittingly may be siding with the Egyptian slave masters—and that puts rather serious, not to say ironic, demands on divine forgiveness.

If God values his diverse moments with each unique group, we may be sadly astray if we are making idols of static rules for uniformity, for we never act in barren isolation.

Here is where the manner in which Joseph Fletcher championed the slogan, "*decide here and now,*" in his once popular *Situation Ethics*, fell short. For at every moment, faith finds itself considering infinitely wider vistas than those of the empirical situation his "new morality" talked about. So our *situation* is itself vastly changed as to the givenness believed for each new here and now.[17] (We are heartened to venture far more deeply into life's

16. See my Karl Barth retrospective, *American Scholar*, i and 108–15.

17. I feel some proponents of so-called *Situation Ethic*s badly misstated their case—as if we should cut loose and grasp the situation in secular terms and then apply a self-exculpatory dodge: "Love is not liking. So just give people what you think is good for them, and we'll call that loving!" Here the love command seems to be reduced to something akin to Kant's rationalistic categorical imperative, as though the love in question makes no crucial demands on the inner heart affections. I wonder, should we water down and slight the daunting inner depth of the love Christ mandates? By the same token, dare we lose from sight the Christ-revealed eternal dimensions of our situation before him? (In view, Fletcher, *Moral Responsibility*, followed by John A. T. Robinson.) See

possibilities than does the shallow libertine myth that has become common in our pop culture. For we find ourselves situated within sweeping promises and unlimited possibilities of faith: "All things are possible for God."

One often meets those who have abandoned themselves to an attitude that tries to sound noble in its egotism, but may actually represent only a sadly diminished resignation: "Well, it doesn't matter what I do, so long as it is *my* own decision—what I choose."

## THE CHIMERAS OF CHOICE AND DUTY

But am I the one who finally *decides* what is to be the shape of some other person's life or what are her true needs that should be served? For that matter, do I even *decide* who I find myself to be or what I find myself wanting to be? Do I have a pedestal apart, from which I can claim original causation and to have determined which of my diverse and ambivalent motives has captured first place in my mind?

As we're reminded by Jesus' parables, even the Reign of God, our highest commitment, is something we stumble onto like a treasure—something that grows upon us from almost imperceptible beginnings even while we're not really watching, with the unobserved inevitability of a seed or bit of yeast even while we sleep.[18] With Luther and Calvin, I would contend that I do not truly decide even my own will in the popular sense as agent.[19] Rather, I discover that what I now want has precipitated from uncontrollable streams of thought flowing in large part from the inchoate reaches of my unconscious. I almost stumble upon my own will in any matter.

---

page 34, footnote 24; p. 62, f.n. 10; p. 82, f.n. 3. The Reformers, by contrast, always began with our new, revealed situation, which challenges us beyond our capacities and at the same time proffers divine renewal that far outflanks our own abilities to truly love without divine acceptance and aid.

Consider here Luther's stress on how we are always taken to task (*Anfechtung*).

18. Mark 4:26–33; Matt 13:24–34; Luke 13:18–20.

19. Compare Rom 7:15–17.

When I do finally come upon it, it is as if it has been lying there, on a rock shelf between the incomprehensibly complex strata of past experience (all the long-since said and done that I don't now control) and an equally complex foreground (including the countless givens, only dimly perceived alternatives, and a shaky guess regarding consequences). As Eastern psychology has long described it, my present decision cannot easily escape or abruptly change the *karma* or inertia of my long-since gradually formed character and habitual attitudes.

As we discover our own will, it may be informed by grace and liberated to the highest reaches of communal hopes, or it may be languishing entangled in lesser desires. But do we really control it? If we regard the self with honesty, I think we must admit that we do not in any simple, practical sense decide the present leanings of our will—at least not in the common sense of full existential control. Rather, the present moment opens onto who we have become, as it were, while our backs were turned—and what weeds and wonders have been growing in us while we've slept.[20] Be all that as it may, the will of the faith-filled person expresses a different self—one oriented to a vastly greater array of reality claims than does the will of one who feels alone and on the defensive.

Without that faith, we believed ourselves empirically bound by our world experience,[21] so insecurity and mutual alienation preoccupied us. Naturally, our mortal fears pushed us to hunker

---

20. Mark 4:26–32; Matt 13:24–30 and 44–46. See both Luther and Calvin's writings, especially in dispute with Erasmus over the popular notion of *free will.*

21. Study will show that an empirically delimited sphere of action is essentially what Paul referred to as the *"life in the flesh"* that is to be opened up to vast new vistas for life to be discovered in company with the Holy Spirit. This has little or nothing in common with the dualisms that are often still confused with it (spiritual vs. physical, mind vs. body, or soul vs. sex). See such passages as Paul's ending of Galatians (5:16–25; 6:8–9) or Romans (7:5, 14; 8:2–16; 1 Cor 2:1–12; 6:17–20; 12:3–4; 2 Cor 5).

By the same token, those "gifts of the Holy Spirit" that Paul speaks of, such as in 1 Cor 12:5, are not to be confused with the notion of some general human quality or "spirituality." Paul is always thinking in terms of actual living intercourse with God himself present and his current gifts to us.

down into a defensive attitude that affected every decision regarding ourselves. So, as the Reformers described it, our wills were (and remain in part) enslaved. Looking back at that state from faith's perspective, we find it hard even to use the words "free will" to describe that circumscribed natural state. Bereft of love's bonded support, we were hedged in by all the ugly delimiting powers of this world. The alternatives to the spontaneous love, in which we all are chosen and to which the gospel calls us, were not life and freedom, but entrapment and compulsion.

Contrary to the aura of looseness or indefiniteness that may seem at a glance to lurk in a seminal ethic of fluid response, the self-bestowing love that Paul and James both call Christ's law of liberty engenders a more explicit living-person response than any canon law.[22] For, from moment to moment, it puts more direct and individualized concerns in my mind than can any set of prescriptions. And there is no hair-splitting casuistry to insulate me from finding myself personally involved at any moment. It becomes far more intimate than the detached rationality of some legally prescribed *duty*. Remember, it is an "unprofitable servant" said Jesus, "who only does his duty."[23]

## LOVE, THE LAW THAT KILLS US

That I must truly love here and now in Christ's uncompromising terms is itself the most excruciating law. There would be no real gospel in it if we were to take the bare love imperative "as our only rule" and the last word for our life together.[24] For, as Jesus himself

22. Jas 1:25.

23. Luke 17:10. It is, I think, instructive that this is the only place Jesus of the Gospels ever mentions the key Stoic (and military) ethical principle, habitual *duty*; and he dismisses it as an inadequate ethical motive (for love serves freely and needs no sense of duty or compulsion.)

24. This is how Joseph Fletcher's once-popular "New Morality" would describe love (Fletcher, *Situation* Ethic.) See page 62, footnote 10 and p. 82, f.n. 3. Since human beings can't fully control their loves, he felt we have to water down the love command to bring it under our mastery. So he put in its place a Kantian rationalism: Do what you supposedly can judge is good for others in

said, making their own lives acceptable to God is quite "impossible *for people.*"[25] But does that mean we should gut the love he will have of its passionate component in order to make it something we can pretend to manage, despite the inadequate feelings that often overtake us? Instead, the unqualified love command seems to press us to reach out, open-armed, toward faith's infinitely larger *situational* horizon praying for the grace we lack: "All things are possible for God,"[26] including emotional refreshment and newly motivated love. "Ask and you will receive, that your joy may be full"[27] (and your eternal alliance will be in force).

It is important to note that in the earliest New Testament text we possess,[28] we find Paul already trying to convey that it is God's power in grace—his active love—that is the decisive source of our life fulfillment, and not our own ability to decide and accomplish—not our teeth-gritting effort and pride in tugging at our own moral bootstraps.

Where Christ's excruciating love command becomes our law, we must cringe at our obvious shortfall. But right here we are everagain caught up in Christ's upward-spiraling drama of grace, as our confession re-encounters God's promise to forgive and heal, and brings his saving gifts back into view.

If it depended on us alone, the call to perfect love, taken as a stark call for our own decision in a human-dimensioned now, would be a crushing imperative. "You must love!" is anything but

---

a mechanical way. (As if your true feelings toward the other could be morally indifferent!) To make love humanly doable, Fletcher tried to flatten our theological situation by declaring that the agape in question has nothing to do with our emotions or heartfelt care for others, but concerns only the outward shape of our immediate actions toward them here and now: "Loving is not liking!" Thus the love command was rationalized into an impersonal abstraction and rendered toothless. I don't know if Fletcher ever came to terms with the resentment you evoke when, without empathy or personal affection, you presume to do what you've decided is good for someone in order to polish your own halo.

25. Mark 10:27.
26. See Mark 10:27.
27. John 16:24.
28. I. e., in 1 Thess.

good news: Count others better than yourself in a heartfelt affection? Embrace not only strangers and refugees, but those who hate your guts? Love your worst enemies and lay down your life for others?[29] That's all?!" "Just be perfect as God is perfect," as the Sermon on the Mount winds up—Is that all?![30]

Uncushioned by Christ's grace as God's forgiving and re-creative promise, this bare call to act out of love can be utterly cruel. "Love!" as a bare command kills all our pretensions. Whenever it is crowed out as a slogan by some church or caught up in the arrogance of a moralistic crusade, it is deadly and spawns illegitimate offspring: In some it gives rise to self-delusion, hypocrisy, and false pride. ("Why don't you people get busy and love like we do?")[31] In others, who are more guileless, it evokes the despair of abject failure. ("How could I ever manage a compassion like that!") I have seen dear ones, overwhelmed by the unmitigated love command, become clinically depressed and suicidal. The isolated command, "Love!" is anything but gospel.

This is serious business, even a public health issue. So this must be of first concern for those called to share in Christ's *healing* mission: Only when his love command is clearly embedded in God's all-embracing grace, does it become life-restoring. We are not to categorize or accuse others with any bare ethical demand.[32]

When we begin with God's grace and continue with his grace—keeping it in focus—our message for the world is patently open, patiently forgiving, and powerfully re-creative. Yet this requires that we always point beyond ourselves to his tenacious grace. When we do, it not only engenders hope, but carries intimations and foretastes of the virtually impossible agape that a loving Lord bestows—something palpable even to our sharp-eyed critics.

29. John 15:13.
30. Phil 2:1–4; Matt 5:44.
31. See Luke 18:10–12.
32. See John 5:45 in the Greek text, where Jesus the healer, who says (as our sole ultimate judge), "do not imagine that I will categorize you before the Father." In this perspective, it does not mean depression, but relief and joy to confess oneself, as the Reformers often put it, already "justified and yet still a sinner [*simul iustus et peccator*]."

So we freely begin each day where, as Christ's Sermon on the Mount declares, we are happily blessed despite our pervasive moral poverty—even while we are still famished, still "hunger and thirst" for the wholehearted love and righteousness that escape us.[33] We are in fact saved and set free by the very love that, known as law, exposes and defeats us.

Here we should notice that although Martin Luther King Jr.'s slogan, that people should be *"judged by the content of their character and not by the color of their skin"* is astute secular politics, it still falls far short of Jesus the Healer's "judge not!" If categorically speaking, Christ will not categorize, then our judging by character is just as unchristian and evil as any racism. (See John 5:45 and Matt 7:1–5.)

## A SEMINAL SOCIAL ETHIC

A typical question from modern sociology needs to be addressed as we approach Paul's free-reception, free-expression schema. It is one thing to speak of our individual interaction with the living One who accompanies us. But isn't it something quite else to ask, what about the formation of society itself? Ever since George F. Mead impressed us with the fateful role social structures play in establishing our self-view, an important question for the New Testament's life teaching faces us here. Can our personal faith response change and restructure our social systems? This has become one of the most pressing questions to Pauline thought—especially where today we have a democratic spread of responsibility for civil law and government across the entire body politic.

Any approach here must be cautious. The road toward Christian social ethics is littered with the booby-trapped wreckage of

---

33. See Matt 5:3 and 6, especially in the Greek text. As I've observed, the church never would have survived if the old saw were true, that its fallible actions would drown out its words. It must always point beyond itself to a love and hope infinitely greater than what is exhibited in its own behavior. Actual hope radiates through any amount of darkness. (It is a genetic fallacy to suppose the church's mission depends on impeccable representatives.)

many reckless attempts to meld church and state, Christ and culture, Christian ethic and civil law, Christ-mindedness, and would-be spirituality. We must remember here that any temptation to *lord it* over the whole of society is a pagan chimera[34] "of the flesh," out of character with life in Christ. Jesus observed that politicians always will want to make their nations and themselves great. But there is to be no confusion of the coercive powers, typical of the principalities of this world with God's power. "It shall not be so among you!"[35] Jesus' stance was typified most clearly in the later Gospel, where he is pictured donning a slave's towel to serve others.[36] Finally he bore a cross, expressing God's passion to liberate them by refraining from a Messianic takeover, such as Daniel had envisioned (that is, to avoid using an overwhelm of divine power in putting things right).

We are misled when the dominant spirits of our society or our own *esprit de corps* insinuate their way into our minds, as if strong feelings of interdependency, or tribal emotions for our own "way of life" (be that German, American, or whatever), could stand in as the voice of God. The disastrously warring "isms" of our own age have all done that: Fascism, Marxism, and consumerism. Indeed church history is littered with the bones of earnestly felt, but disastrous heresies which came from claims for the Spirit's leading, in contravention to our only norm for discerning the Spirit, which is and must remain a question of coherence with Jesus' own life and teachings.

This is why Karl Barth felt pushed to declare that the only true sacrament[37] is the Christ of Scripture. The Holy Spirit's continuing presence can be recognized only where there is continuity with the

---

34. Mark 10:42–43. Consider the kind of temptations pictured as rejected by Jesus (Matt 4 and Luke 4).

35. See Mark 10:35, Jesus' response to James's and John's request for greatness.

36. John 13:1–17.

37. That is, following Augustine's classic definition of a sacrament as "an outward and visible sign of the inward and invisible truth."

life and teaching of Jesus Christ. He remains the one crucial norm for any claim to spiritual discernment or guidance.[38]

But more needs to be said, or we might be left with the kind of two kingdom split which permitted many German churchmen simply to give over temporal state powers into Hitler's hands unchallenged. For the truths of God's incarnation are to extend as far into this world as any believer can influence the structures of state or society.

Two things should be especially noted here. First, there is a new communal context (that of belief: "Thy Kingdom come") which can, and gradually does, become the effective social frame of reference in which the believers know themselves. Self-knowledge and values are not independent of society. Our humanity *in Christ* is itself corporate. The network of our social consciousness and interdependence is infinitely greater than any world power, and so we are called to think beyond the narrow strictures of tribe, nation, or culture. Yet, there is a beautiful paradox here: We are at the same time called to be exquisitely concerned for and responsive to the least individual.

Paul was speaking theologically, and not just working out missionary tactics, when he told the Galatians that he had become as they were in order to reach out to them. The covenant community in which one comes to a renewed self-awareness is not to be culturally Greek or Roman (or American).[39] For viewed "in Christ," it includes already *all*, without being subject to the cultural arrogance or the idolatry of any dominant group or agency. (This means we are not to hunker down in a defensive nativism or be swept away by any competitive siren call to make our tribe, our Reich, our Caliphate, or our America "great again.") "Whoever would be first among you must be the servant of all."

Second, Paul left faith's expression through political action a free possibility, wherever or whenever a believer is in a position

---

38. See Paul's radical claim: "Whatever does not proceed from faith is sin" (Rom 14:23), or Jesus' vine metaphor, "Apart from me you can do nothing" (John 15).

39. Gal 3:28; Rom 10:12; 1 Cor 12:13; Col 3:11.

to affect society's general patterns or civil law and to help bring about change. It remains important to notice, however, that here as in all else, the Apostle felt no compulsion. He felt no binding imperative to impose Judaic law upon his Hellenistic hearers.[40] Instead, he let the Torah itself be supplemental and marginal to their Christian calling, although he gave them plenty of indications that it remained holy, just, and good as God's free gift for a liberated people.[41] By the same token, Paul did not load down Gentile converts with traditional halakhah or legal interpretation.

## PAUL AND THE LIMITED ROLE OF LAW

Paul believed that the law, properly grasped, describes a freely-covenanted responsive life. But for him, it remains a resource for prudential use. With Jesus' words, "you have heard that it was said of old . . . *But I say* unto you," ringing in your ears, even the Hebrews' ancient nomadic ceremonial can have transfer value if you translate it into current expression forms. But it is implicit that anyone in a position to affect social customs or civil laws would want to consider their underlying significance and purpose

---

40. Indicative here is the Philemon text, which is the accompanying letter Paul wrote for the runaway slave, Onesimus, to present on his return to his legal owner. Both these men have found their way into Christian faith. So Paul suggests that despite the empire-wide iron-fisted sanctions against runaways that they, mindful of the liberating grace of Christ, are free surreptitiously to ignore the Roman law's gruesome sanctions against a runaway's theft of himself. He does not ask them to shoulder the impossible burden of changing the Roman Empire's law all by themselves. He does, however, suggest that they avail themselves of the first opportunity for a legal manumission. But in the meantime, responsive to Christ, they are free to work out an unheard-of *modus vivendi* together and act as virtual brothers.

Indeed, the common Hellenistic practice of ritual manumission becomes Paul's key metaphor for atonement. (The bill of sale attesting that money had been paid into some shrine for the deity's virtual purchase became, in effect, an ex-slave's certificate of having been bought free.) For Paul, Christ's costly self-spending, by analogy, becomes the symbolic surety of our ultimate liberation.

41. See e.g., Rom 7:10–16; 1 Tim 1:8.

without being wedded to outward forms. For Jesus' "But I say unto you" evokes ever fresh response.

Sacred law as an abstract description of living covenant for liberated community, then, remains a backstop. But where the man Jesus Christ, has stepped into the foreground, he has become the liberating norm. For those who have his freely proffered suffering service in view, he himself became the clearest, most accessible portrayal of what grace-responsive life is and must be (along with the resurrection promise, that God would not let him, his way, or his loved ones simply die).

So for Paul, Jesus himself pre-empted the role of law in confronting believers' lives. The Lord's example and teaching are at once simpler, more coherent, and more explicit than the law. But beyond that, his life has made clearer than ever before what the prophets had long discerned: The formal outward performance of rules is not the goal of God's "*thing*."[42] As said, Christ's life as model also becomes an overwhelming norm, as does his law of love—deadly, if we aren't mindful that the purpose of such diagnosis is that we be drawn toward his grace and eager for his freely channeled forgiveness and renewal.

It surely has been no surprise to the Liberator God that people invariably fail his *Dabar*, whether stated as law or embodied in Christ.[43] So he must intend something more than ape-like conformity. Has he not, all the while, been evoking living relationships that have passed through the crucible of heartfelt frustration, repentance, and yearning?

The higher goal even of the ancient Hebraic law and sacrificial system was to be grasped as God's initiative not to coerce conformity, but rather to engender and reinforce our freely bonded interdependent communion. Paul saw it all targeted on a vivid experience of loyal love and mercy and embodied in a joyfully sabbatic covenant. Yahweh had always been after a wholeness

---

42. Hebrew: *Davar/Dabar*, God's "*thing*," his purpose or word, was often identified with the holy Torah's law.

43. See Rom 11:32.

palpitating with heartfelt immediacy which could never be reduced to a set of outer forms.[44]

Again, as Paul saw it, "Jesus Christ is the end of the Law" in a multiple sense. For him the reference to Jesus as Christ is inclusive of the whole corporate "body of Christ." By "end" Paul seems to give full play to the pregnant meaning of that word: both as the Law's goal, purpose, and meaning certainly, but as its final termination and higher replacement, as well. For Christ himself has become the law's visible embodiment. So Paul was stressing two things.

First, what God promises through Christ is the most full and literal fulfillment—the end goal—of the community that the Torah described. As Karl Barth pointed out, what is humanly visible in Christ has become the only clearly visible *sacramental* appearance of the life attitude and quality of community that the law had commanded all along. In Jesus Christ *finally* God's will was shown in uniquely case-specific, audio-visual concreteness.

But second, Christ also becomes law's end goal, not just by pre-empting its normative role, but by replacement: transmuting its final judgment (within the heat of God's own passion) into an ever-new promise of forgiveness and re-creation imaged in the symbol of Christ, the healer, envisioned at the right hand of the Father as our life's sole judge.[45] Thus *promise* is in command: "You are to be—you are going to be—perfect as your heavenly Father is perfect."[46]

---

44. As I mention elsewhere, the Reformer, John Calvin, reflective of Paul, makes a theme of how God asks of us the very things he well knows that (given who we are) we *cannot do* in order that we might see *what we should ask* of him. That is, the experience of our impossibility has a divine purpose. For it bonds us into the kind of grace-based companionship that finds a prime expression in prayer.

45. According to Mark's Jesus, he finally claims this role "at God's right hand" as his own at his trial (14:62), and Luke has him mention it in a final discourse as a role to be mediated by his apostles (Luke 22:30). The spread of references shows this image of Christ the healer as our only final judge, and it was given key importance across the entire early church. See Heb 1:3; Rom 8:34; Col 3:1; Eph 1:20; 1 Pet 3:22.

46. Matt 5:48.

Here I would repeat and stress that in the apostles' view, isolated outward behavior is not the final goal of Christ, who is the living law. Life's goal is covenanted relationship—the personal life address of grace-responsive persons. So Christ would never dominate human beings or manipulate them. Neither would he ever override the most fallible "little ones" in their innermost tender selves with grandiose social agenda: "Who made me a judge or divider over you? . . . Judge for yourselves what is right?"[47]

Here I'd hasten to stress once more that appropriate communion with Jesus Christ does not shrink into slavishly aping his two-thousand-years-distant behavior. That's not what the believer's inspired *imitatio Christi* need mean.[48] For Christians' action was always a matter of following along with him who is present as Spirit, according to Jesus' parting, "Lo, I am with you always."[49] We may believe he will remain true to himself right through an array of circumstances vastly different from those of first-century Palestine.

Again, possession of newly revealed insights does not mean Paul's followers should simply ignore the ancient Hebrew law. Yet he realized that the mere possession of such legislation, however right and good in itself, could never empower its own fulfillment in the sort of radically liberated community of grace that it mandated. Paul's attitude toward his own earlier rabbinic existence was an expression of this realization, although he admitted to no break with Judaism. Yet Paul's reference to how some believing Jews "killed the Lord Jesus, as they killed the prophets and have persecuted us as well" (1 Thess 2:15) shows that he was fully aware that possession of good law does not in itself insure a good life. As said, the bare love command empowers neither the loyal affection (*chesed*) it mandates nor love's heartfelt contributory justice. What it does is diagnose our need.

The early Paul of Thessalonians does not yet show us his most mature claim for grace, whereby Jews as subject of God's covenant

---

47. Luke 12:14, 57.
48. Eph 5:1–2; 4:15–16.
49. Matt 28:20; 18:20; John 14:16–18.

are *already* saved—analogous to how children may be unconscious beneficiaries of a trust fund set up on their behalf—and may still be unaware of how great a role sheer grace has played toward their promised heritage.[50]

Given his Christ-enhanced grasp of the Torah's holistic corporate intent, Paul saw only self-delusion in his own early zeal as a Pharisee to establish a Jewish order under law.[51] Now he would take the Torah's history to show that good law serves primarily as a backlight: It diagnoses the human condition by casting actual human relations into dark silhouette. That whets the appetite for a fulfillment that people can receive only as a gift in the full light of grace. All this becomes excruciatingly clear when the law is understood to mandate Jesus' truly holistic love, preferring others to self[52] and extending to the worst-case offenders and enemies.[53]

If like the rich man in Mark 10, you blithely say you've managed to keep law and are already the kind of person ordained there, Paul, like Jesus before him, would probably have been too kind to call you a damned liar.[54] But he would have you ask yourself whether, like him, you've not been mired in self-deception. "For people it's impossible," Jesus had declared, but our possibility is penetrated and outflanked by God's unlimited potential.

Paul repeatedly reminds us that all have sinned and fallen short, where God's right, good, and just liberty-defending law of love is concerned. Wouldn't it be like flogging a dead horse to flail away with the law that has defeated us? Yet, thank God, the assurance of the accompanying Spirit who was introduced to us in Christ begins to awaken in us the very love and social harmony that have escaped us. Faith's awareness of his loyal presence as

50. See Gal 3:15–4:2.
51. N.B., Gal 1 regarding his zeal.
52. Phil 2:3–4.
53. See 1 Pet 3:19–20. Jesus' "descent into Hell" has become an apostolic symbol for Messiah's grace reaching out to embrace the worst cases imaginable of degradation and evil.
54. Paul does slide into his roughest language for any who dare assume superiority and discourage others by foisting legal prerequisites onto them (see Gal 1:8–9; 5:12).

Spirit gradually inspires, motivates, and finally will evoke in us the very attitudes the law required. Against such "first-fruit-of-the-Spirit . . . there is no law."[55]

## PAUL'S TRUST IN FREEDOM, A SCANDAL

Someone once noted that you can understand what is important for a man by observing the enemies he makes. Paul was hounded throughout his ministry by a group of opponents. These were a vocal minority among the first Jewish-*Christians* who found his open life teaching so scandalously risky that they hounded him from place to place, warning against his liberated ethic. No doubt some traditional Jews, still untouched by the Jesus movement, would find Paul's liberating message intolerable on the same grounds.

There were of course a number of related issues, but Paul repeatedly was forced to defend his gospel against some of the worst misunderstanding. So important was his passionately Christ-centered faith that he was willing to suffer harsh persecution and imprisonment over the issue. One of the accusations which Paul found most damaging (and repeatedly defended against) was the charge that his flexibility regarding the law was but a craven license designed to ease his way and make points with the Gentiles.[56]

But the accusation that Paul had been making the moral life too easy is to be understood in large part as serious complaint against the conceptual structure and form of his teaching and not just an accusation of slackness or neglected standards. It was his marginalizing of accomplishments associated with being loved and accepted that stuck in the craw of the "false brethren," the Judaizers he knew as Pharisaic Christians, or the "circumcision

---

55. Gal 5:22–23.

56. Aimed against just this accusation is his repeated reminder that, though he was collecting financial relief for Jerusalem, he always had earned his own income and purposefully abstained from monetary support (1 Thess 2:9). The same thrust is behind that astounding passage where he feels forced in self-reference to rehearse "like a madman" the list of harrowing ordeals he has suffered in order to spread the gospel (see 2 Cor 11:7—12:13).

party."[57] They objected to his reduction of the rules to which one must refer every action. In short, they were dead-set against Paul's easily comprehended micro-ethic which no longer would saddle people with complex ritual, legal systems, or daunting catalogues of virtue.[58]

The Pauline approach to life was pithy with strong, simple outlines. It did not require a complicated philosophical or religious-cultural background—not necessarily even that of the Torah law—in order to be assimilated. Largely for this reason it was transferable to all kinds of people of diverse background. This, of course, helps explain both its rapid incursion into the Hellenistic world and the resentment of some nativistic Jewish[59] and Jewish-Christian opponents.

That the following generation would find some things in brother Paul "hard to understand"[60] is a testimony to how estranged even some Christians would feel from the Pauline emphasis that full freedom comprises obedience to the imperative of grace, although there was really nothing very complex or abstruse about it.

---

57. Gal 2:4–12; Acts 15:1–5. These critics claimed to be zealous for Jewish tradition, as Paul describes himself to have once been (Gal 1:14).

58. See Rom 7:6.

59. See, e.g., Acts 23:12.

60. 2 Pet 3:15–16.

# 4

# OUR LIFE IN GRACE SPANS TIME AND SPACE

Paul's practical exhortation was quite intentionally capable of ever-new re-application and flexibility for changing cultures and circumstance. It was not as though he were claiming to have a preset rule or something definitive to say in the disposition of every case, but quite the opposite: he was trusting others' walk with Christ. So what he had to say about behavior was utterly simple and at core intimately personal. People needn't be learned to grasp it, yet it pointed them far out beyond their own capacities to something much fresher than their own best motives—far richer in its available resources than their own self-centered will to be good or great—far more promising than any congregation's actual moral tone.

> For freedom Christ has set us free; stand steady then and don't let anyone yoke you back into slavery. (Gal 5:1)

If you have been living in constant confrontation with conflicting values and pluralistic opinion, can you find a center that will hold? This was a persistent problem for people living in the culturally diverse Hellenistic and Greek cities of the first century, and it framed Paul's ethical task. As a Hellenistic Jewish rabbi, who was also a Roman citizen moving about the Empire, he confronted a bewildering diversity of mores and values in conflict. (Note that our intercultural experience today parallels his own, often at an even higher level of intensity.) The remarkable simplicity of the gospel's new life-guidance system that emerges in Paul's letters (still as a kind of minimal seminal ethical core) is apt to be clouded over for us by the complexity of the conflicting ethos and value systems that people in his new, culturally mixed congregations had been pressing him to address.[1]

Paul's letters, for the most part, take up actual problems of practical confusion and hot issues of value conflict that have been brought to him with an urgent request for his opinion. It is almost with reluctance that Paul, feeling his way toward the present implications of the Christ claims (or "kerygma") he had received, suggests Christ-appropriate approaches they might bring to their current experiences.

As all students of Paul know, we must read between the lines in his responding epistles if we are to understand the actual questions that had been posed to him by members of the congregations he had founded. If we fail to appreciate the pressure of their clamor for his opinion, we may find it hard to grasp how someone who made others' freedom his life slogan could be so ready to lay out for them his own opinions about behavior.

But if we remember Paul is responding freely to his friends' pressing requests for a frank response, we won't presume, as some still do, that he was trying to lay down a new law for all time. In those utterances, such as Galatians 4:12, where he urges others to

---

1. The immense popularity of mystery cults, burial societies, syncretistic philosophies, and gnostic sects in the first-century cities witness to the cultural unease of peoples whose native identities and beliefs had been shattered by successive waves of Greek and Roman occupation, which had given rise to a widespread nostalgia for a lost sense of identity. It is an anachronism to suppose that the defensive cool of Stoa or the thought-cocoon offered by Neo-Platonism had issued in a quiescent, tolerant mood (thus Houlden, *Ethics and the New Testament*, 21). Even in Greek cities, issues of social displacement and intercultural confrontation were strikingly analogous to those we experience today.

be as he is, Paul had already become notorious for advocating full freedom.

He of all men is the partisan of a radical, new liberation doctrine.[2] Audacious freedom in the face of legal requirements had become the line most tightly tied to Paul's name; and this had become a widely publicized scandal in the eyes of Judaizing Christian opponents who branded him as a dangerous revolutionary.

For Paul to say, "Be of my own opinion," can only mean, you may be just as free of any compulsion in your own interaction with Christ as I am notoriously free in mine. It can't possibly mean he'd have them ape him or even try to mimic Jesus in new situations.

The problem situations they pressed Paul to address were complex with subtle political and cultural overtones. But his responses (although they open up to speak to and embrace in affection a diversity of value conflicts) show him to have been remarkably focused in purpose; for he would see their old situations trumped by faith's new situation "in Christ." Such re-visioning (or "repentance") brings all their differences into relationship with a pervasive life-center.

Paul believed the personal heart of God's grace to be so luminously visible in Christ that people may sight it with clarity from any number of different viewpoints. Thus, it gave orientation and direction to people who had been ensnared in the various moral confusions that arose between competing lifestyles, needs, and drives (the sort of identity loss and value conflicts that were rife between the divergent tribal cultures, philosophies, and cults of the Hellenistic and Greek cities).[3]

---

2. Pagan participants in Paul's wholly voluntary, grace-based associations did not have his religious tradition behind them. So, it would have been a graceless presumption for him to demand their submission to his will.

He did not think of himself as demanding submission, but as encouraging them, so they too might discover in Christ their own liberation from whatever authoritarian compulsion had entangled them in the past. Any attempt to force their minds anew with a compelling message (or message of compulsion), he knew would ignore Christ's good news and be an "accursed" distortion, even if it should come from him or a "messenger from heaven," such as Moses (Gal 1:6–8).

3. It should be noted here again that, for us, to be "scriptural" in our

## RESPIRATION IN THE SPIRIT—"RETURNING GRACE"

As we have been seeing, there is a great simplicity in Paul's grasp of new life—a simplicity which at moments of rediscovery has ever again become the catalyst for reformation and renewal. For Paul any life which has become responsive to God's own gracious freedom, where he is himself in and through Christ, has two phases which can neither be separated nor reversed in order. The very outline of Romans, which contains the closest thing we have to a connected essay on Christian existence from the apostolic church, follows this pattern: Everywhere we look with Paul, Christians' life is described either in its reception phase as a grace-gifted or—in the whole-hearted personal engagement it evokes—the spontaneous "fruit of the Spirit."[4]

As mentioned above, these two phases of faith's experience of "life in grace" (or more accurately of God's grace active in our lives) in practice meld into a self-reinforcing upwards-tending spiral. Here we find ourselves in a pulsating life drama. We are challenged by his love and aspire to embody it. Yet falling short, our very lack prompts prayer and new beginning as we ever again repair to grace. Thus, we find ourselves cheered and challenged in a motivational cycle that actually draws us upward. Yet infinitely more important than any marked progress is the life-fulfilling fact that we are here finding ourselves permanently bonded into the gifted, inter-personal covenant that is at play from first to last.

The resilient priority of grace has often been obscured in Christian ethics, as if the whole life discovery could depend on the quality of our own responses. But Paul saw the believer embraced by God's unwavering purpose. His sovereign initiatives in grace that swirl us upwards are never caused by the quality of our

---

methods must imply that we share the Christ-centered openness to diversity that is manifest in the canon itself. I remember hearing Karl Barth, certainly one of the most biblically grounded theologians of the last century, exclaim with a chuckle that Scripture itself must contain a couple of hundred different theologies.

4. See Gal 5.

preparation or conditioned by the adequacy of our response. To be sure, his gracious presence will inevitably spur some graciousness in us, but that so-called *growth* remains secondary and subordinate in the process of new life.

As said, this order is irreversible: Only as we first find ourselves drawn into his presence can we rediscover who we are and are to be, or find the readiness to express it. "Apart from me you can do nothing!"

The life response of Christians is real to the extent that there is belief—belief in a living God who is actually present and, as such, none other than the resurrected one of memory. Our expressions retain vigor through all vicissitude and change to the extent that we have felt free to return ever again to our source in the givenness of his life for us where he maintains our unearned legacy, a place forever in his limitless grace.

This means our new corporate life is to be grasped in its entirety—not just in its first inception or in its final fulfillment, but as a storied whole. The dimensions in which we are wholly conscious, wholly active, and most decisively ourselves are here embraced in the larger action whereby God is insistently himself, creating us as one eternal corporate body, wholly interdependent, living consciously within the eternal matrix of his grace.

Paul used two intimately linked terms to express this unity of the new life as God's single creation. When the sixteenth-century Reformers went back to Paul, they found they wanted above all to rehabilitate the insights behind these two terms and to clarify the irresistible, gifted progression of the new life they describe: *justification* and *sanctification*.[5] Together they denote the one inseparable and irreversible movement of God's Spirit, as he *adopts* us as his own, communicates new life to us, and re-creates us to fill the place he holds open for us.

---

5. These linked terms unfortunately have become less familiar today. Perhaps this is because the particular faith claims to which they refer seem themselves so unlikely from the standpoint of our everyday competitive struggle, where people scratch away for security with little sense of life as a freely shared gift.

We have described above the initial discovery and constant communion phases of Christians' lives, as Paul saw them. The contents of his prominent words *justification* and *sanctification* correspond. The justification of our lives is their gifted, intrinsic worthwhileness, the divine purpose by which our existence justifies the air we breathe and the space we occupy in God's community now and forever. Paul sees this fully as a given, an inalienable grace, because it is ascribed to us in God's love for us. Hence, it has become as much part of our identity now as our name, as much a gift as our original birth or adoption. It denotes the permanent substance of our total personhood with divine sanction behind it. We are the creatures whose existence, for better or for worse, God justifies simply out of his grace. So it refers to an unqualified *full* status that is permanent by virtue of his sovereign purpose and restorative power. No wonder Paul uses the imagery of *adoption*, *election*, or *engrafting* for our gratuitously ascribed identity here.

## GRATITUDE: THE IMPERATIVE OF GRACE

Paul's most important insight for our subject comes to a focus in the phrase that John Calvin always used to summarize Reformed thought here: "those God *justifies* he also *sanctifies*." A single sovereign purpose is constant behind both aspects of new life. Through Christ God draws his people to discover a permanent relationship and therein inspires actions that more and more bespeak the mature wholeness of their promised community. The first aspect, *justification*, is unqualified and permanent as God's own sovereign "yes" to our lives as wholes. This becomes visible to us only as we find ourselves receiving a share of his vision, through faith.[6]

---

6. Although Paul is translated a few times here with the shorthand expression *justified by faith*, an expression that has become a slogan, the actual meaning is the justification of faith or given to us through it. Our believing or trusting is in no sense the cause here. Rather, God's own initiative is the instrumental cause: we are justified *by his grace*—a gift we may discover and accommodate in faith. (Compare Rom 8:30 with 5:1, where the Greek, εk, is often misread as if our faith were the final cause, and 3:28, where *pistei*, may be misread as a dative of instrumental cause.) The later church wrongly began to

But inevitably along with the awareness of the living God's justifying embrace, we find new motivations taking form within us. Through this new motivation, he begins to give new form to our behavior in all its dimensions. So where justification is a once-and-for-all gift, *sanctification* denotes the equally gifted sequel—the movement of grace-expressive moment. As we find ourselves reoriented to faith's apperception of reality, new and appropriate motivations take hold by fits and starts (never as a glossy completion). Our reception of faith's reassurance will be spotty—always somewhat fuzzed up by static from the hedged-in and ego-bound atmospherics of ordinary experience. Our sanctification, however, comprises in aggregate—all the scraps of faith hope and love, all the worth-while moments we've shared with others in anticipation of everlasting relationships.[7]

In other words, as we are given faith and discover justification irradiating our lives, new affections are evoked under title of filial love, gratitude, and joy—new actions of grace. These certainly are self expressions and one hundred percent one's own. Yet they have been motivated in and by extraordinary claims that have taken us by surprise. It is part of that surprise that millions of us quite rationally find ourselves actually sharing the hope and belief that all this is not simply the product of wishful thinking, but at root the gift of God.[8]

Still, it would be quite flat-footed to hold that justification and sanctification relate to each other *only* as psychological stimulus and response. New motivations find us already living on the level of personal conversation with the gracious Lord, as he is believed to be present with us. We respond directly in company with him, currently "in spirit and truth" and not simply to the received idea that we are imbedded or engrafted into everlasting community.

---

turn this sovereign gift into an iffy business, often misreading and mistranslating the texts. (See, for example, how a text such as John 15:10 [that in context stressed God's initiative] has been punctuated to connote the very opposite: as if God in Christ can love us only if we first manage to obey and conquer our non-love.)

7. 1 Cor 13:13; Gal 5:22.
8. Eph 2:8.

We find ourselves sharing his concern for others and their needs, but this is much more a question of total person orientation and awareness than it is a closed cycle of motivation response. We've noted how Paul uses the imagery of the whole self being "engrafted" into relationship with Christ and his community here leading to *"fruit of the Spirit."*[9]

Unqualified, justification does not depend on how complete or fully "formed" the sanctification of a Christian's life in this world has been or ever will become. Here the Reformers, returning to their sources, discovered Paul had been ignored and overwritten by less hopeful traditions in the lore of the medieval church. Almost buried was Paul's confidence that our full permanent value does not depend on how fully we find ourselves already enabled to reflect that love, which in its very essence must be gifted, spontaneous, and free.

And yet equally important in the Reformers' recovery of Paul was their confidence that a gradual renewal of life would actually take root in believers' lives as actual re-creation begins to take hold. For as Calvin would stress ever again, "those God justifies *he* also sanctifies."

The Heidelberg Catechism exhibits how this awareness came to resonate through the Reformed tradition: Here the whole of Christians' life is presented under the rubric of *Dankbarkeit*, person-engaged *gratitude* and *thanksgiving*. All our interactions and our personal obedience are to become, as Calvin's French idiom had it, simply a matter of "returning grace."

According to Paul, that very first halting prayer, "Abba, Father," wherein we Gentiles began to intuit that our very identity is to be discovered within his love, not only points us to a complete and permanent gift (*justification*) but is in itself a harbinger of the way the Spirit's presence will continually influence how we speak and live. (*sanctification*). Consisting for faith in actual, free

---

9. Gal 4:5–6. and 5:22–23. The Fourth Gospel attributes an analogous vine-branches imagery to Jesus himself (John 15:1–5, 16); and there is a wealth of further imagery connoting intimate personal relationships: adoptive *"children of God"* and *fellow heirs, chosen bride, or friends* of Christ, *ransomed slaves*, etc.

interaction with the Holy Spirit, this life-embracing eternal relationship dawns on our awareness with that first, wistful sigh of prayer, "Abba!"—"Look, Dad, if you're really there to care . . ." A door has been opened for good upon a permanent Presence. We will always recall having stretched out open arms and murmuring, "Abba, Father," toward the unseen Spirit, who has been claimed to be like Christ in his humanity toward us.[10]

As said, the two phases of the one gift of new life are inseparable, as a personal unity, yet irreversible in our lived drama. "Those God justifies he also sanctifies." The whole dynamic is a gift in faith lodged from first to last in the living priority of God's grace. Believing God as the "source of all goods," as the Geneva Catechism has it, Christians are motivated to honor God by irradiating a heartfelt thankfulness.[11]

The bishops at the Roman Catholic reform Council of Trent (1545–1563) sadly failed to jettison decisively the medieval accretions which had bogged down the gospel message in the speculative notion that justification must depend upon our prior behavior (the cart before the horse) as if *justification* were to be purchased by our *sanctification*. People's ultimate status or worth here seemed

---

10. Gal 4:3–9. It is noteworthy that Acts 2 traces the birth of the Christian church for some members of the Jewish Diaspora to that Pentecost event, when like an electric current or "flames of fire" enthusiasm swept through them as they listened to the Galileans' claims. We should note that God's presence as Spirit was nothing new to any Jew. They had long believed him able to hear prayer and inspire the prophets. But astounding was the new insight into *who* he was—if he actually had represented himself as Messiah among them, paradoxically revealing himself as not other than the crucified and resurrected healer of memory. This was a revolutionary claim to be thrown open to all the world on their return to their own synagogues. (Their fluency in one of the three great lingua franca of the day is implied by how their home regions are listed in Acts 2:8–12.)

Paul traces the inception of the church for his Hellenists from the similar moment when any of them had reached out tentatively toward the previously unknown God (as the Spirit who made himself known in the Christ message) and first murmured, "Abba, Father." For those of us who are Gentiles, then, such would ever again mark our beginning in the church, just as that Pentecost had been its birthday for diaspora Jews.

11. Calvin's Catechism of 1542, Qs. 3–7.

to hang in question until they had earned it, completed a virtuous preparation, or at least been white-washed by the accumulated merit of the church.

The counter-reforming conservatives fatefully won the day and ensconced a darkly medieval distinction between your *preparatory, unformed faith* (which they saw as a necessary prior achievement), whereby you *may* finally manage to shape up and embody the fully *formed faith*, as if you needed to win over a reluctant God.

Only after violent dispute between the Bishops at the Fifth Session of Trent did the medieval conservatives gain the upper hand and vote to canonize their notion as official Catholic dogma. In the minority bishops' opinion, this was an anti-christic disaster, since it implied that our adoption by God is a grudging and iffy concession that leaves our final acceptance uncertain—as if his love depends upon our legal score card.

The Reformers protested:[12] this was the very opposite of gospel. For where insecurity and doubt were allowed to cast a pall over life, either a pharisaic pretense of self-righteousness or an abject despair hovered near at hand.[13] So Trent's distinction between *fides formata* and *informata* had a leaden ring in the ears of those newly re-attuned to Paul's gospel.

In one of Charles Schulz's cartoons, Charlie Brown's friend Linus asks the obstreperous Lucy: "When you get big, do you want to be somebody great?"

"That's an insult!" she shoots back.

"An insult?"

12. See especially Calvin's *Institutes* III.ii.8 and the tract he wrote as an "Antidote" to Trent.

13. One can ask whether this has not in fact been reinforced by a tendency toward institutionally fixed and controlled canon law, on the one hand, and the temerity to write off unbelievers, on the other (by assuming an exclusivist superiority and rejection of outsiders quite foreign to Paul's teaching and Jesus' own spirit). Similar popular speculations regarding one's permanent status before God crept back into the Puritan churches later with the so-called *syllogismus practicus*, the graceless notion that you can dismiss some as reprobate to God if their practical behavior remains reprehensible. Here again Paul's gospel was swept under the rug.

## OUR LIFE IN GRACE SPANS TIME AND SPACE

"Yes, I feel that I'm great already!"

Lucy could be almost Pauline,[14] if her discovery of prior inalienable status were lodged in God's universal grace (rather than in her own ego). But the insult involved (as Paul would see it) is really an offense against God himself—when we pretend that God's love is reduced to the scale of our paltry accomplishment. To do so makes our lives unroll in an illusory frame of reference. So, our deference makes a difference.

In what follows, we shall look more closely at how Paul's seedlike ethical teaching unfolds evoking heartfelt prayerful practice. But a couple of cautions are in order.

First, in examining the mainsprings, there may be a danger that we satisfy ourselves with mere formula and become forgetful of the kaleidoscopic refraction of his faith's light, with each believer's unique interaction with the Spirit present. Let us agree that as we summarize, we are only describing the genotype, as it were, from which creative and diverse flowerings will spring evergreen.

We should also keep in mind throughout that the Bible never divorces people's actions from God's ongoing action as lifegiver. Any human freedom is his concurrent free gift—that is, it is grounded in the self- and world-determination of God's own action. It is his freedom both to grant and delimit our freedom. In short, there is no Christian ethic to be found apart from theology (or more properly, apart from Christology).[15] In Paul's Trinitarian terms good life in God's good creation can most clearly be experienced as life *in Christ*—that is, in relation to his grace-pledged community of belief.

This does not mean that this "good" may not be believed by us for others (as objectively good *for* them) and even *on behalf of* others (in their place, so to speak). But the basis for Christians'

---

14. It strikes me as amusing that this same dialogue took place in the 2016 presidential campaign, when Donald Trump boasted his neo-fascist-tinged claims to "make America great again" and Hillary Clinton countered that he was being insulting, since "we're great already." Sad to say, neither candidate's notion of American exceptionalism seemed particularly grace-informed.

15. This theorem has received its fullest recognition in the theology of Karl Barth.

action remains in and of faith's interpersonal intercourse with God. So though a derivative morality might take hold as a sort of spin-off in a "Christianized" cultural milieu, the social ethic will rapidly lose its coherence and its heart and meaning if morality is cut off from its sources in a living faith relationship.

# 5

# PAUL URGES: THINK ON THESE THINGS

## "YOU FILL IN THE BLANKS!" (PHIL 4:8)

There is an especially telling word toward the end of Saint Paul's letter from prison in Rome to the Philippians. This passage is often seen as a *catalogue* of prescribed *virtues*, as if he were following a common Stoic pattern.[1] But attentive reading suggests

---

1. People often posted so-called *Haustafeln* in their homes, tables of ideal virtues for emulation.
See Houlden (*Ethics and the New Testament*, 19, 23), who like many sees similar lists of virtues and vices in certain Pauline passages, such as Col 3:5—4:1 or 1 Cor 6:9. But although Christ's love means respect and understanding for all things human, the present passage, with Paul's evocation to consider "*whatever* is currently thought virtuous," shows he was thinking of a Christ-responsive freedom that is the *very antithesis* of a preset list of virtues prescribed for all times, places, and situations. The works of Stanley Hauerwas show how you can and should give full attention to appropriate virtues while remaining quite clear that we cannot "know beforehand for all times and all places what set of procedures or practices will insure [Christ's kind of] justice" (*Christian Existence Today*, 13).
Hauerwas's long-held concern to describe specific virtues in Christian's life certainly has a place in ethical reflection, and Moltmann's criticism may

that he intended something far more interesting and indeed quite revolutionary.

Despite his plight as prisoner, Paul stresses repeatedly how life in Christ resonates in a mood of playfully light-hearted joy: "Rejoice—again I say rejoice!"[2] Then in chapter Four, we have *in nuce* his stripped-down final word, his whole *ethic* if you will, for an inwardly free life of direct person-response.

Here is his summation, as I would transcribe Phil 4:8– 9:

> Finally, for the rest brethren, whatever is deemed "true," whatever is thought to be honorable, whatever "just," whatever "pure," whatever is considered "lovely," whatever "gracious"—if there is anything generally thought to be excellent or virtuous, anything considered worthwhile—pay attention to such things [ταῦτα λογίζεσθε].[3]
>
> But what you have learned and received and heard or observed in me, do. Live like that. The God of peace is going to be with you.
>
> I rejoice greatly in your renewed support.

Note what needs to be clarified is that Paul is not referring just to Jewish mores here, but to whatever qualities your own or your

---

be overdrawn (*Ethics of Hope*, 33). But there is a sense in which a traditional Methodist focus on outer behavior risks losing the Reformers' acute realism about the simultaneous shortfall of our lives as Christians. As Hauerwas would remind us, to dwell on "the confrontation between these constructs of ideal types [virtues to be possessed by church people vs. others] is abstract and impracticable."

From first to last, Christians should be pointing past themselves, confessing the corporate shortfall they share with all others before a divine imperative that "is impossible for men" (Mark 10:27). Instead, they are to point past themselves to God's grace for all, as known in Christ. We might do well to recall Calvin's frequent reminder that since living personal relationships are the gospel's concern more than outer patterns of behavior, even the strongest "virtues" possessed by alienated persons remain, in effect, vices so long as they equip and strengthen their egos in a sadly self-defensive independence.

2. Phil 1:19; 2:2, 18, 28–29; 3:1; 4:1, 4, 10.

3. Some would translate Paul's verb here as "calculate," but in context it would be better expressed as "be cognizant or aware of," or simply "consider" or "bear in mind." He is speaking of a warm, even positive recognition, not a coldly calculating analysis.

## PAUL URGES: THINK ON THESE THINGS

neighbor's background culture may find agreeable or acceptable.[4] So he lists a string of widely used terms that, in the common lingua franca (of koine Greek), were broad enough and fluid enough to carry quite different implications for each of the diverse religions, philosophies, or cultures his readers might confront among their Macedonian and Hellenistic cities' diverse populations.[5]

Bearing in mind that, in all Western history, this was a time most like our own in terms of mixed-culture populations, look more closely at his word choice here:

ὅσα ἀληθῆ [*whatever* strikes people as true]

ὅσα σεμνά [*whatever* seems seemly]

ὅσα δίκαια [*whatever* is considered just or righteous]

ὅσα ἁγνά [*whatever* is thought not to be base or smutty]

ὅσα πρσφιλῆ [*whatever* people hold to be lovely or beautiful]

ὅσα εὔφημα [*whatever* is spoken well of]

εἴ τις ἀρετὴ [if *anything* is thought to be virtuous or excellent][6]

εἴ τις ἔπαινος [if *anything* has a good image or reputation]

ταῦτα λογίζεσθε [think about/be attentive to/consider these things]

Paul is saying that, no matter what a person's background or cultural context, if she is indeed a free agent, joyfully liberated in Christ's love and eager to share God's peace with others around, she will want to be realistically aware—tuned in to such things, both in her own and their backgrounds. Respectful of human values she

---

4. Karl Barth reminds us that Paul's call to be attentive to whatever *government* is in force (Rom 13) is one instance in his thought of the flexible consideration he urges here. See further below.

5. Compare Thurneysen, who says, "Here I declare myself solidaric with others beyond the church" (*Der Brief des Paulus an die Philipper*, 143).

6. This is the Hellenistic word for *virtue* or *human excellence*. That Paul leaves its contents completely open and flexible ("*whatever* people consider virtuous") is further evidence that this is not listing a preset *virtue catalog* of mechanically habitual behavior patterns.

## NEW TESTAMENT MICRO-ETHICS

may remain, as Jesus himself once put it, as discerning as a serpent, yet as harmless as a dove.[7] Yet it would be unwarranted to jump to the conclusion that Paul supposed either we or others, by taking thought, would be empowered to accomplish such human ideals, for even the finest human ideals become a frustration. Whatever their background, all share the same need for a power beyond their own human frailties: a cosmic healer.[8]

As we've been observing, it is not that Paul's new gospel is weak or flaccid in its ethical implications, but quite the opposite. He sees companionship with Christ as affecting every practical decision with direct immediacy, and that for him is what makes actions truly human. As said, Christ's grace invites and liberates commensurate, personal responses, each original to our particular social or intercultural moment. This means we can be holistically engaged with people, wherever they are, without dumping further legal baggage or pre-scripted programs upon them.[9]

I might be tempted to dub this *situation ethics*, except that when Joseph Fletcher popularized that term as a "new morality" for the 1960s,[10] he tended to ignore, or perhaps simply sadly failed to clarify, how faith's belief-orientation to our shared place within God's grace[11] becomes the prior, all-embracing *situation* that trumps the more limited dimensions of our experience—whether natural or cultural—to both liberate and condition all our actions.[12]

---

7. Matt 1:16.

8. Compare Ellul, *To Will and to Do*, 60 and 281, n3. It is suggestive that the pericope about Jesus and the woman taken in adultery ["Let him who is without sin cast the first stone!"] evidently was treasured in the oral traditions of the mixed congregations of Asia Minor long before it was attached to their Fourth Gospel (John 7:53–54). Even by their own standards, people of every background experience the need for healing.

9. Rom 7:6.

10. See page 34, footnote 24 and page 82.

11. Again recall that the first word in relevant texts, *metanoio* (an about-face, or positive re-orientation) is usually translated in our texts rather too narrowly by the regret-laden word *repentance*. (See page 24, footnote 5 and p. 82, f.n. 4)

12. See e.g., *Situation Ethics: The New Morality*; Robinson, *Honest to God*. See pages 31–32 with footnote 17. Wesley Baker's *The Open End of Christian*

PAUL URGES: THINK ON THESE THINGS

## ALL THINGS ARE LAWFUL, BUT . . .

No matter how values may change, as one moves between cultures and groups in a pluralistic world, there is always a question of simply showing respect and kindness and not giving offense which takes on vital missionary force. As a former Pharisaic legalist, the bottom line here was revolutionary for Paul. On occasion he would exclaim, "*All things* are lawful for me!" And he meant it quite literally. After all, the whole "earth is the Lord's and everything in it." And it only underscored that the flexible freedom and precision Paul had been finding here is really that all-inclusive when he went on to explain that this did not mean he, being free, would find any old thing equally helpful and up-building.[13] His responsive freedom to say yes was also a responsible freedom to say no.[14]

For Paul, however, there is to be no compulsion as if we must, on the one hand, fall in with every current social idol or tattoo ourselves with every pop practice, or on the other, ape him (or slavishly imitate even Jesus). But he finds us to be gifted with the freedom to express grace in creatively adaptive forms—forms which may remain fluid from culture to culture. A Christian's open intercourse with other persons is always a present calling, and such cross-cultural accommodations as exhibit our freedom will have overtones of mission.[15]

---

*Morals* did well to grasp our situation in relational perspective (see 111 of his book) though his talk about making "moral persons" may have obscured that he was describing grace-responsive life, and not a self-absorbed conceit that we can actually remake who we are as persons.

13. 1 Cor 10:23–26. See also 9:19–21.
14. See my essays on *Liberating Speech*.
15. Some, uncomfortable with Paul's openness to pagan values and practices, think it more likely that he is in effect cheerleading his addressees to conform to the virtuous, and commendable qualities in his own Judeo-Christian tradition (see, e.g., Grayston, *Letters of Paul*, 43). But while Paul's prior Pharisaic use of Old Testament law is certainly included in the wide scope of his words, "whatever is excellent," both his intended audience here and his notoriety for liberation teachings (which evoked violent opposition among, those he calls "Pharisaic" Christians, "Judaizers," or "false brothers") show him most deeply concerned for cross-cultural and interreligious openness to

## NEW TESTAMENT MICRO-ETHICS

My friend Don Harris, a retired diplomat, describes how beginners in his profession must learn that even similar values and commitments may be quite differently expressed in different societies. So when you cross borders, you should be just as ready to exchange your coin of expression as you are your money. As world-travelers must learn, this is true even on the superficial level of common etiquette. Consider a couple of home-spun examples:

A frontiersman may have avoided tobacco all his life, but he would have thought twice before refusing, out of fixed principle, to puff the peace-pipe offered him by a neighboring Indian chief.

I grew up in family whose tea-totaling rule was quite practical. (If *as settled principle* you never drink, you testify to the danger of alcoholism and run no risk of becoming a drunk yourself.) But when I went to Scotland for my junior year of university, I learned that a quaff of wine was at the very heart of the Scots' First-Footing custom, a festive New Year's ceremony expressive of family- and friendship-bonding. So was a remote risk of alcohol abuse to outweigh the immediate offense of refusing their glass of hospitality?

Again, I had always been taught that to show regard for a lady, you should help her with her chair at table, open doors and step back for her to enter first, and hold her coat for her. But as a grad student in Tübingen, when at a dinner table I pulled out a lady's chair for her, she jumped aside and wheeled on me, with a startled, "Oh, you wanted to sit here?!"

Or when I would start to step back to let a German friend enter a cafe first, I would feel her hand in the small of my back propelling me in ahead of her. (It seems the German swain was to stride in first, hand on sword-hilt, to see that all was safe there for his lady.) And yet again, on returning to America, I had to learn that for quite different reasons, it was no longer a sign of respect to be opening car doors for athletic young co-eds. To treat anyone

---

"that which is generally accepted as right conduct" (Lohse, *Theological Ethics of the New Testament*, 2). Paul's attention to others' values here is even more outward-tending than the bare golden rule, which asks us to take self-regard as a norm for our conduct.

attune to women's lib like a fragile flower had become the very antithesis of personal regard.

Forms of speech, of course, are deeply implicated here. In Europe it used to be something of a ceremony when two acquaintances would first begin to use the familiar forms of address with each other, for it implied a pledge of lifelong friendship and commitment. (And of course to address anyone else with the same familiar pronoun would show contempt.) A young Danish doctor told me that to pretend to more than three or four such friendships not only exposes you to an overwhelming personal burden and risk of loss, but is downright immoral, akin to infidelity. In traditional Sweden you addressed ordinary social contacts obliquely in the third person and used titles: "Will the Herr Professor have a cup of coffee?" But in reaction, perhaps, a modern generation has reversed all that. When during a sabbatical in Finland we enrolled our daughter in a Swedish school, she had to learn to address even her teachers familiarly, by their first names, ostensibly as a modern sign of friendly respect. By the same token, in pluralistic America first-name familiarity has become a general social lubricant and is a comfortable sign of congenial respect.

Paul as a Roman citizen who had grown up as a Jewish Pharisee in Tarsus, a very mixed Hellenistic city, was quite aware of shifting mores, where the outer coin of expression differed from group to group. He was quick to acknowledge that grace will find ever-fresh ways to express itself, whatever the going coin for reflecting the kind of loving and up-building regard that has claimed you in Christ—be it giving a cup of cold water in character with him or by carrying out the trash, drying the dishes, or loading them in a dishwasher.

That free transfer between different coin of expression characterized Christians from the beginning. On the Pentecost that we celebrate as birthday of the church,[16] Diaspora Jews were lingering in Jerusalem after their once-in-a-lifetime pilgrimage to the temple-crowned city, the symbolic heart of their identity as the liberated folk of the Exodus. Pentecost for them was *Law Day*. It

16. Acts 2.

followed the liberation celebration, Passover, after an appropriate time as a celebration of God's further gift of his Law for a liberated people.[17]

For the earliest Christians, Law Day was recycled or superseded as the Day of the Spirit. The wonder they experienced here must have been far more exciting and revolutionary for them than mere belief in the presence of the Holy Spirit. (After all, Jewish belief in God's accompanying *Shekinah* was as old as their wilderness sacrifice cult—in fact as old as prayer itself, which would have been meaningless without belief in God's spiritual presence.)

The real wonder here at the church's birthday was that a group of pilgrims from polyglot "Galilee of the Gentiles" were so very intoxicated by Christ's expansion of the Passover's liberation message, so emboldened by news of the suffering Messiah's resurrection, so possessed by the sense that God's presence as Spirit was not other than Christ's Spirit tendering his gracious healing and liberation for the entire world. Astounding—a bit embarrassing, perhaps! Though the pubs weren't even open yet, as Peter pointed out, they were so drunk with the message that they were bending the ear of Diaspora pilgrims on the eve of their journey home— sliding into the common Greek or Latin of people's home synagogues, if these were outside their own Aramaic sphere, in order to declare God's gracious new initiative for them all.[18]

We can be sure that for Luke, in writing about it, the real, all-important miracle was the glowing claim that God himself is for all and that his Spirit's presence to all is now to be known, as not other than that of Christ. The true wonder was what moved them: that his Spirit would be embracing the whole world through them, as the rest of Luke's account in Acts will attest. So the saving message itself was the miraculous thing, and not particularly the mechanics of its transmission, however supernatural they may or may not have been.

---

17. That is, after a full seven Sabbaths beyond Passover (7 x 7 = 49 days), the fiftieth day (Pentecost) celebrated Moses' receipt of the Liberator's law.

18. Note again that the places mentioned in the text are grouped according to these three dominant language areas (Acts 2:9–11).

"When in Rome, do as the Romans do." That saying is commonly and mistakenly attributed to Paul. But it is still rather appropriate: You're free to express yourself with sensibility for Roman behavior patterns. We find him saying something quite similar in his letter to the Galatians: "Brethren, I implore you to become as I am; for I also have become as you are."[19] If such flexibility is called for where simple etiquette is concerned, how much more important it must be where we are expressing our heartfelt response to the One we find loving us all in Christ. In view of Paul's background as a legalistic Pharisee, this kind of transcultural openness amounted to an astounding liberation. What an enormous verve and new departure he must have experienced! Yet finally, as I have stressed, this new microcosmic ethic ("What you have . . . observed in me, do") with its right-now, whole-person-responsive expressions, could be much more precise and case-specific than any bulky list of casuistic prescriptions.

By contrast, applications of casuistic law or prescriptions of habitual virtues always make do with generalizations extrapolated from past cases that give the outward impression of similarity. But here Paul was talking about discovering the once-and-for-all irreplaceable (and in divine perspective everlasting) gifted uniqueness of each moment in our living relationships—notably including our transcultural ones—following in company with Christ. Of course, as said, faith's grace motivation always will include a missionary concern here that others may discover and enjoy their potential in an equally unique and, as such, everlasting personal response that the Lord embraces as fully their own.[20]

Reformed theologian Karl Barth wrote a study on Philippians during his most significant years of disturbing rediscovery. There he drew attention to Paul's urging that we freely "consider" the traditional *notions of virtue* and the like that happen to be in force around us. Yet in his vast multivolume work that followed, he only mentions the concept *virtue* a couple of times in passing.[21] So

---

19. Gal 4:12.
20. See 1 Cor 9:19.
21. See Barth's 1927 lecture, *Eklärung des Philipperbriefes,* and his *Church*

clearly, he did not find this freedom compatible with the Catholic tendency to put prescribed canon law at the center of ethical reflection, and neither did he nurse a sanguine confidence in the nurture and habituation of a fixed set of *virtues*.[22]

Years ago when I first read Barth's commentary on this text, I wrote this impression at the foot of the page:

> Always in a moment—always in a *new* moment! There can be no repetition. But that means living friendship, as opposed to a mechanical program. The Kingdom of God is neither a policy nor an organization. It is a friendship—a family of living respect.

Where Paul in Philippians 4:8 says only "*consider* these things," Barth had already come to see, as he put it, that Christianity is not ethics and neither does it have a *particular* ethic. As a Christian one can only consider what everyone has to consider. Christianity is awareness of God and even, given its knowledge

---

*Dogmatics* III.4, on p. 620.

22. This approach to Christian ethics has colored in particular some Methodist programs for behavior. Compare the extensive works of Stanley Hauerwas who, though he was deeply appreciative of Barth's methods, settles into the freedom of virtue formation as his remedy for an even more mechanical legalism. N. T. Wright, too, will observe that "Paul does indeed teach what we may call a virtue ethic" and "believes in moral progress with *agape* as the prime virtue." But I doubt if he sees the virtues Paul would have us consider in Phil 4:8 so much as a pre-scripted agenda as a flexible missionary concern. And I don't think he means to stress the root meaning of the word, *virtue*, which implies a habitual agency of *vir*, man, rather than the current motive power of God's grace (*Paul and the Faithfulness of God*, 374–75). In a somewhat similar passage in 1 Thess 4, where Paul had early urged works of love in the broadest terms, he had already framed his paraenesis with the telling observation of "You don't need to have anyone write you" with this, "for you yourselves have been taught by God to love one another." (That is, he finds he can only reinforce and encourage their own quite personal, direct response to Christ.) See also 2 Cor 8:21. The urgings of Col 3 and 4 apparently have the same purpose. Here the writer explicitly contrasts his encouragements with the demands of those who would "pass judgment," "disqualify you," or require that "you submit to regulations" rather than live in free interaction with Christ. (See further Col 3:11 in context.)

about the command, "Christianity is not ethics"—not in the common sense of the word!

So when we in turn ask what Paul's so-called virtue catalogs entail, we must recognize that he saw his converts' behavior in terms of their own freely bonding personal relationships expressed in the most diverse cultural coin. Appropriate forms for behavior, then, always remain a current, live question: What will your neighbors find to be respectful and loving expressions toward them?[23] Freely reflect upon their views; consider their sensibilities; be mindful of their common currency of propriety.[24] Then, as Paul says in the next breath, when in affectionate freedom we commit to action, what we actually do as followers of Christ may be something quite else (Philippians 2:9). What shapes that something else?

---

23. Compare Verhey, *Great Reversal*, 70–71, regarding "the natural and human moral wisdom . . . which may be utilized and even esteemed."

24. Rom 12:17. Compare Ellul, *To Will and to Do*, 77, 93, and 106.

# 6

# IN CHRIST, BE YOURSELVES

## WHAT YOU HAVE OBSERVED IN ME, DO! (PHIL 4:9)

What are we to make of it, in our Philippians text, when Paul goes on and apparently intending a strong contrast says that while we will be attentive to the widest diversity of mores and attitudes and give them our full consideration, we actually are going to be guided, finally, by something quite else? What else?

> What you have learned and received and heard and seen in me, *do* [πράσσετε]; and the God of peace will be with you. I rejoice in the Lord. . . . I can do all things in him who strengthens me.[1]

The young Karl Barth, as he came to terms with Paul's contrasting "do" here, burst out:

> Do! Do what *you*—what in the moment is asked of *you* . . . [It's not a question of what all the others have been asked to do.] You are to do—do what you . . . *You* . . . (Otherwise it wouldn't be you doing!) Do what is asked

---

1. Phil 4:9, 13.

of *you.* [Uniquely *you,* here and now, in this living moment:]
  The *thankfulness* [as expressed in Paul's nearby verses] and his, *Do this!* are never to be found far apart: . . . The God of peace will be with you. He is the God of the thankful, the God of the doers of the Word.²

So Barth was learning that for Paul, believers' Spirit-led action entails the frankest spontaneity. Christians' obedience, paradoxically, is always fully free—always a fresh, immediate, grateful person-to-person attentiveness. And he would remind us that in freely expressing ourselves, in constant conversation with God's accompanying Christ-like Spirit, we are going to discover the unencumbered, light-hearted joy that Paul's letter breathes from beginning to end.

As we've noticed, some suppose Paul was presenting himself as a role model to be imitated.³ But, as said, Paul was notorious among his peers as the Pharisee who had changed his spots and championed a great reversal in his approach to the very Torah Law which had been so central to his own rabbinic tradition. As a result, he was in fact hounded by Judaizing *Christians* who kept hurling accusations of wishy-washy inconstancy.⁴

So when he here says, "what you have learned and received and heard and seen in me, do," it can only mean you may discover your own freedom in the gospel, just as I have found mine. That is, you'll find freedom in your own response to Christ to be your real and unique selves—whom you'll discover yourselves to be in him, just as I have found and been myself. How others' concerns

---

2. Barth, *Erklärung des Philipperbriefes,* 123. Barth would come to grasp ever more firmly that our living correspondence with the God of Peace is the context and motivational ground of Christ-appropriate action. For our response follows in a sequential order that may never be reversed. Renewal and salvation are sheer gifts and not somehow merited or earned as reward. See my book *American Scholar,* 214–15, and 222–23.

3. Often it is supposed that an *imitatio Christi* imperative underlies Paul's actions, as if he thinks that if his readers will mimic him it would amount to a second-hand imitation of Christ. (See, e.g., 1 Cor 4:16.)

4. See especially Gal 2:4.

## IN CHRIST, BE YOURSELVES

will affect your own behavior is something for you to work out in conversation with him.[5] Remember Paul is the one who said, "all things are lawful for me," though they aren't all helpful (1 Corinthians 10:23).

We should notice in passing here that Paul's attitude toward the strictures of tribal ethos or claims put forward for a natural ethic echoes the open poise he urges elsewhere as Christians' appropriate attitude toward different governments and their various civil law codes.[6] That is, Paul urges one to be cognizant of them as an always ambiguous, often duplicitous, part of God's fallen world. You will want to be aware, regard such criteria kindly, and bear them in mind. But your actions are to be your own response to God's grace in your political moment, freely supporting the government's function to protect people's peace and covenanted freedom. There need be no friction here—unless government itself has crumbled into its very opposite and become at root evil, tyrannical, and oppressive.

So, when it came to actual doing, Paul would feel free to sidestep or challenge laws not upholding gracious justice and respect

---

5. If Paul was offering himself as a role model, it was only in this inverted paradoxical sense. For he had always presented himself as living in free, direct response to his gracious, liberating Lord. So imitation here can only mean, "Be *free like me*. Be yourself, in your own response, as you have seen me being free in mine."

We saw above how Paul would be freely considerate of both his Jewish peers' and his Hellenistic neighbors' values and ways of life. Since you share that freedom, you may be graciously attentive to others' traditional values. Go ahead now. In company with Christ, your freedom will decide how their concerns are going to affect what you do in company with them.

N. T Wright also argues that Paul is encouraging his converts to find their own Christ-responsive way, rather than pressing a prescribed canon upon them. It misses the genius of Paul's reference to intracultural diversity to suppose with Houlden that, despite his critique of legalism, "he puts forward rules and lists of moral norms" (*Ethics and the New Testament*, 118). The quality of responsive relationship that Houlden otherwise stresses remains key throughout, so the expression forms, virtues, and norms that he urges remain rather malleable, and (this author does note) did not intend a precast rigid canon.

6. This perspective may cast light on the much-disputed political ethics of Romans 13.

for all. Nevertheless, being free in grace, you don't have to waste yourself in quixotic rebellion. For example, you may begin to treat your slave owner or your legal slave as your brother in Christ and equal,[7] despite the empire-wide established law, even though you are not yet able to avail yourselves of legal manumission. For bottom line, in Christ there is no slave or free, no rich or poor, neither Greek nor Jew, neither male nor female, nor any of the other value categories that alienate us—neither oligarchy nor meritocracy![8]

Again, just as Jews' and Christians' awareness of the Holy God is not based on experience of ordinary Nature (but yet entails a new, infinitely enhanced valuation of Nature as God's good creation, and respect for natural science as well), we have here in the social arena a parallel instance of the same attitude: Our liberated response in action is not based on anyone's claims for a nature ethic or for natural-law. Neither is it grounded in any taken-for-granted mores or tribal values. In our sin-shot mortal existence such things are always ambiguous and duplicitous. Yet since our faith entails gracious respect of others, we will be cognizant of and respectful of such claims' importance to them. Nevertheless, we will be responding freely all the while in faith's own direct, freshly creative and kindly critical ways.

In other words, natural theology must give way to a theological grasp of Nature—which for us may well mean grace-responsive ecological action.

---

7. See Phlm and 1 Cor 7:21–22. Distinguish these from other texts which, focusing on the mission impact of socially acceptable behavior, perversely forget to insist on slaves' and masters' full equality and seem content to urge them to use their freedom to fulfill their officially sanctioned roles without a hitch (e.g., Titus 2:9; Eph 6:5; Col 3:22) But it totally misses the radical new departures of Paul in Philemon, his theological application of the symbols of ritual manumission, and his frequent call for freedom to suppose, as many do, that for Paul slavery as an "institution goes unquestioned." Nowhere are Christians' life responses simply spiritualized. "For freedom Christ has set you free, stand fast therefore, don't submit to a yoke of slavery" (Gal 5:1). That would become revolutionary at many levels.

8. Rom 10:12; 1 Cor 12:13; Gal 3:28; Col 3:11–25. Compare John 5:45, where Jesus says, "I will not categorize you." Have we recognized that categorizing by merit is just as alienating as by race?

## IN CHRIST, BE YOURSELVES

By the same token, Natural ethic must be held in abeyance to a theological grasp of human values and interaction.

Though we're minded to give others our full attention, we are not inwardly bound by general notions of natural law or by taken-for-granted mores. We will tender such claims regarding natural and traditional virtues as important human constructs. Yet as part of God's beloved but sin-shot creation they are always ambiguous and duplicitous. So experience of Nature is never to found, fund, or delimit faith's present, living response to God-with-us as Person or our witness to his grace for all persons in Christ.[9]

When I first pointed out the New Testament's micro-ethic phenomenon,[10] my longtime colleague Allen Verhey was apprehensive that this observation might detract from the imperative force of Jesus' ethics, which indeed are supercharged through what Verhey called a *"great reversal"* of Messianic expectations. Jesus' teachings and self-bestowal do core right through all outer forms into our innermost motivation. But our freedom to respond spontaneously out of love remains closely guarded throughout as God in Christ veils his awesome power. So we would stress again that Jesus' reluctance to dictate elaborate rules for behavior belongs to the great reversal, which Verhey so forcefully portrayed.[11] We might do well to share that reluctance.

It should be clear that the force and final precision that can shape action are not weakened here, but heightened and tightened. Christ-responsive liberated persons care, and they take care in their actions. Yet as Philippians tells us, we are under no compulsion or paralyzing pressure. Instead we may respond in a peaceful mood. An attitude of refreshment is warranted with heartfelt

---

9. Houlden does well to point out that for Paul, received "virtues and duties were not only to be transcended," but could be "condemned as the occasion of pride" (*Ethics and the New Testament*, 19). This insight became prominent in John Calvin's Reformed critique of the medieval church's moral theology. (See, e.g., *Institutes* II.ii.11; III.xiv.3.) Yet as we have seen, Paul would nevertheless encourage us to give them our free and gracious attention.

10. I was suggesting this perspective already in the early 1980s, notably in a paper for the Society of Christian Ethics ("Corporate Selfhood").

11. See in Verhey's solid initial study, *Great Reversal*, 70.

gratitude, rejoicing, and good-humored confidence—even when our surroundings are hostile.

Without doubt, the ethical brevity and transcultural fluidity we've been observing here are among the things that explain why the new faith (as we can well believe, nudged along by the Holy Spirit) jumped so rapidly across diverse religious and cultural frontiers and in just a few years took hold in the life of every nation. Such solidarity with those of diverse cultures and religions still liberates Christians' speech and action today.[12]

## THE LIBERATING ETHIC UNFOLDS AS SABBATIC LIFE

The blare of trumpet or ram's horn echoes across the rooftops as the sun sinks away; all work and striving cease, and the quiet repose of God's Sabbath takes hold. By the same token, three thousand years later, Sunday church bells ring out to embed each week's work in a Resurrection Day's gifted relaxation and peace, and in Muslim villages a Muezzin's voice cries out for pauses that recall each part of every working day to God's embrace.

In whatever form, the sabbatic pause that punctuates Scripture's grasp of all life as a gift is far more than a work-supporting recess for rest and playful recreation (though that basic restorative need is, of course, to be met). Our entire life—if it is to embody its truly human and fulfilling purpose as envisioned in Scripture—is to be lived in confident sabbatic relationship with the Life-Giver. Under analysis Jewish, Christian, and Islamic ethics unfold as basically sabbatic in their style of life. Here is to be found both glorious profundity and refreshing simplicity by contrast with other life teachings.

As Rabbi Evan Moffic likes to point out,[13] the flexibility of a seminal ethical core, such as Paul derived from Jesus, was already in the air for many within the rabbinic Judaism of their day. The

---

12. This is a key theme in my essays entitled *Liberating Speech*.
13. Moffic, *What Every Christian Needs to Know*, 95.

## IN CHRIST, BE YOURSELVES

noted Rabbi Hillel famously opposed Rabbi Shammai just here. In a legendary incident, Hillel rose to someone's impudent challenge that had enraged Shammai: "Can you recite the Torah while standing on one foot?"

Hillel responded with a form of the golden rule: "That which is hateful to you, do not do to your fellow. That's the whole Torah; all the rest is commentary."

Obviously, Rabbi Jesus of Nazareth in his summation of Judaic law was equally ready to begin with a seminal ethic epitomized, first in the words of the ancient Shema, "Love the Lord your God with all your heart, mind and strength," and then, attune to that, "love your neighbor as yourself."[14] This was deeply rooted in their ancient sabbatic faith.

As Rabbi Moffic puts it, "Following and expanding upon Hillel's perspective," Jesus too would "focus on the person over the procedure, the felt needs over the legal precedent."[15] This approximates what we've been stressing as immediate, person-responsive freedom, over against all kinds of prescribed ethical programs.

A rather typical commentator would have us suppose Paul is saying that "all that is necessary, is to have a few *settled principles* on which one always acts" and that one's mind "ought always to be occupied with pure and elevated thoughts."[16]

Well, yes—Paul is pointing to a simplified orientation, equally effective in any given time or place. But to equate that with "*settled principles*," I fear, may have it upside down and backwards. His *principle of Spirit accompaniment* is *flexible* enough to be personal, dynamic, and timely. But it is not *settled* and fixed, as are abstract principles. Incarnate, it is his glory to be engaged in our ordinary mundane concerns and not only with "elevated" matters. Finally

---

14. See Mark 12:28 and parallels; here Jesus was citing the Hebrew Schema (Deut 6:5 and Lev 19:18).

15. Moffic, *What Every Christian Needs to Know*, 99.

16. Scott and Wicks, "Epistle to the Philippains," 118 (italics mine) Contrast Ellul's flat-out declaration: "There are no Christian principles. Most of the heresies came into being as a result of transforming the word of God [who is a living lord] into principles" (*To Will and to Do*, 204).

whoever would be great must become the servant of all; for "whoever exalts himself will be humbled."[17]

Note the ethical response is Paul's concluding word in his appeal to the Philippians, and not his first; he intends to remain in strong contrast alongside his openness to others' mores: "*Finally, for the rest, brethren.*"

Having exhorted free, open-ended conversational behavior, he concludes his seminal ethic by inviting them simply *to follow*. For him our readiness to follow will unfold as a result of and sequel to the gospel's promised assurance, and in no way can be its prerequisite, preface, or ground.[18] Paul is pointing to a living accompaniment—to the Person, in whose believed presence we will ever again respond freely, hopefully, prayerfully, gratuitously, creatively. That actual and conversational response means tighter, more rigorously case-specific expression in action than any pre-fixed *settled* principles can engender. To have epitomized and internalized the ethic like this in no way weakens its creative power for even the smallest minutia in life.

---

17. Mark 10:35, 43–44; Matt 23:2; Luke 14:11, 18:14.
18. Phil 4:9. See Thurneysen, *Der Brief des Paulus an die Philipper.*

# 7

# ETHICS STRIPPED DOWN FOR THE WORLD

## TRUSTING FULL FREEDOM—OURS AND OTHERS'

It could not be my intention in this short book to describe Christians' specific actions, as they unfold ever-new in their rich array. I will suggest in closing, however, a few highlights indicative of the *sabbatic life* we've been describing, where the Apostles' simple *seminal ethic* unfolds for us into a many-splendored diversity. Like Paul in his letter to Galatians, let us trust our own and other Christians' fullest freedom, as we discuss creatively how best to serve and respect each other, even though the ways we've taken may diverge.

The finding throughout this essay on the New Testament's condensed seminal ethics has not been that the Christian believer has little life guidance, but quite the opposite: Instead her or his whole being is directly, responsively, and creatively involved in the life of all those around. She or he remains free in discovering a realistic, respectful, and practical timely expression toward the others in full consideration of their reigning customs and values, whether those be Jewish, Hellenistic, Roman—or for that matter, Polynesian, Martian, denominational, or pluralistic. It is a stripped-down, highly flexible ethic that we find in the New Testament.

Again, this in no way implies that the gospel must be devoid of finely tuned ethical implications. Again, the very opposite is true: For Christian faith affects every human action, shaping our behaviors directly, appropriate to each new milieu where we may find ourselves. Our mission will ever again evoke an immediate response to new persons. Since we are free to recognize and use the coin of self-expression already familiar to them. Spirit-led, we will respect and remain adaptive toward their mores. Let me stress it again: From the beginning, Christian ethics were to be dynamic and fluid—creative and new in each new meeting—without having to drag along a bulky canon of casuistic precedents or pre-set program for behavior. Since faith itself is sabbatically person-responsive and not legalistically fettered, our every moment of meeting, every handshake, every caress is invested with the promise of unique eternal consequence. For the life-preserving, everlasting God has made himself our constant companion as Spirit.

In Galatians (Paul's Magna Carta of Christians' freedom) he has an apparent contradiction: He says believers, of course will be carrying one another's burdens. Then, in almost the same breath, he says that being free, they will each wind up carrying only their own load before the Lord.[1] The apparent contradiction melts away when we consider that in context Paul is urging Christians to trust their own and each others' full freedom. Each person's actions—at least in her freely grace-responsive moments—will open

---

1. In Gal 6:1–6, where Paul describes how we carry one another's burdens [τα βάρη] freely out of love's compassion, he uses a simple, matter-of-fact present tense. Motivated by his love, you simply do carry [βαστάζετε] each other's onerous burdens. But to describe our own accumulated *backpack* of weighty life [φορτίον], he uses the future indicative of simple promise [βαστάσει]. The ultimate worth or *pondus* of our lives has not come about as a high-pressured imperative, but is a grace-gifted personal package, so to speak, shaped by a lifetime of trusted freedom within his grace. As such it has unique, eternal substance.

to others, in company with the Spirit; and this will become part of an irreplaceable drama, as we might say, with her name attached. For the Life-Giver treasures her whole life story in its grace-embedded uniqueness and will somehow preserve it as such. We may trust each other's freedom without foisting our own patterns upon those around. Free, open discussion is enjoined, but finally, others' freedom within his covenanted community is to be trusted alongside our own. The revealed claim that we are to be trusted in Christ founds and funds our own freedom. By the same token, we are to respect and trust each other's freedom in Christ.

Their shortfall, along with our own, is being outflanked through a common drama of confession and restoration. It is the paradox of paradoxes that this very drama tightly bonds our permanent grace-dependence—even as our deepest evil or sin—with all its symptoms (distrustful fears, resentments, defensiveness, and the like), is being overtaken by re-creative love and our energy is being recycled (as it were) toward gifted life renewal.

We can observe how the seminal, nuclear ethical implications of the simple kerygmatic gospel proclamation unfold in different historical and cultural contexts and blossom out into a kaleidoscope of diverse forms in every case to be grasped as deeply joyful, packed with everlasting dramatic significance and great joy—often with effervescence and fun.

That Christians' ethic remains stripped down for new action, then, does not mean it is flaccid or vague, but quite the opposite: Sabbatic, pneumatic, holistic, it engages the self in current conversation with God and with others in spontaneous response, knowing each other, as we are known, beloved in Christ.

Let us finally rehearse some core characteristics of the nuclear ethic, as it unfolds in all its person-distinctive freedom and diversity:

## 1) Love-Responsive Life—Sheer Gift

*Obedience* here means to find ourselves enabled by God's grace to be attentive, to hear positively with unfeigned frankness in non-phony response.² This can denote only timely, wholehearted willingness and can never be grudging decision. It finds us. We discover ourselves becoming attuned to something beyond ourselves, hopefully by God's action rather than making a pressured decision. It is more discovery of something that happens to us, rather than program for self-enhancement and control. "For it is by his grace you are saved, through faith; and that is not your own doing. But it's a gift of God; lest anyone should boast" (Eph 2:8). Our own wholeheartedness is a gift which escapes our willful self-control. This realization was central to the Reformers' rediscovery of Pauline thought Characteristically, Calvin emblazoned his personal crest with an open hand proffering a heart aflame under the legend, "*prompte et sincere*"—immediately responsive and wholehearted.

## 2) Grace-Situated Life—Reorientation as Motivation

Christians' new life springs from a re-orientation of the whole person which is intrinsically moving and motivational.

What I have been describing here, I suppose, could be loosely called a "*situation ethic*"—but only in the sense that we have discovered, as our truly all-embracing believed situation, that all are one in Christ.³ Here the gospel's first paraenetic word, *repent*,⁴ meant we are urged to *reorient* our entire existence to this

---

2. See Karl Barth's "Word-Study for Americans" in my book *American Scholar*, i, 70, 108, 114, 163, and 356. I rather suspect that our objection to Barth's continual stress on *obedience*, which began to sound apodictic, coercive, and wooden to our American ears, led him to make *true freedom* the leading motif for his American lectures in 1962.

3. See page 31–32; p.34, footnote 24; p. 62, f.n. 10.

4. As I have mentioned before, *metanoio* means essentially a *mental shift* or *reorientation*. It is only a side light of this full reorientation to the gospel's free grace that it evokes regret and remorse for how we have been hopeless and graceless along the way. It upends the gospel to interpose the notion that God's grace and forgiveness are subject to and depend upon anyone's *prior penitence, acts of penance,* or *rituals of absolution*, as church members sometimes have done. (See page 24, footnote 5 & p. 62, f.n. 11.)

discovery: faith's distinctive life matrix—a new life vision. Every contact between us may be grasped as securely and permanently embraced by his grace.[5] Our situation is always located within the interdependent community of grace-liberated people that was prefigured in the Hebrew Scriptures' pledged covenant. The celebrated *sabbatic interdependence* upon the Life-Giver, exemplified by the saga of the liberating God of Exodus, became normative for the Children of Israel. Jesus said, "Unless you become as children" (and unless *in this way* your rightness exceeds that of the legalistic Pharisees) you'll never be in accord with God's reign.[6] This reorientation becomes motivational and inevitably affects everything we do.

## 3) Sabbatic Life Means True Comedy

Jesus' revelation roots into this sabbatic view of life and would be virtually unintelligible without the Hebrew Scriptures behind it.[7] For example, it was no accident that Jesus' tension with the Sadducees' legalistic ethic would on occasion focus in on the underlying meaning of Sabbath-keeping. For Jesus the sabbatic life stance

5. That is, each situation, in its turn, is believed to be bounded by and understood from a Trinitarian perspective.

6. Luke 9:47–48; 18:17; Matt 5:20; 18:4–5; John 3:3.

7. Attempts to separate Jesus' ethic from its OT roots (such as Marcion's second-century heresy, which was reintroduced by some anti-Semitic fascists in the 1930s) tend toward an unreal, spiritualized view of our basic humanity. At the same time it is essential that the man, Jesus himself, be seen as God's self-revealing Word, cradled (as Luther would say) *within* the scriptural text, or as Calvin would put it, the optic through which the rest is to be grasped. Otherwise, what "you have heard it said of old" confuses what you may believe about the constancy and priority of God's grace. See for example how Jacques Ellul's notion of revelation spread across the massive Scripture is led by such texts as those demanding the *herem* sacrifice (the cruel total annihilation of enemy peoples) to struggle with the notion of a tortured separation between God's own inner nature and the humanity manifest in Christ (*To Will and to Do*, 200). A temporary suspension of the ethical, such as was epitomized in Kierkegaard's famous reflection on the pledge-breaking demand for the sacrifice of Isaac, may be grasped as a significant preparation for God's self-revealing Word without being confused with its substance.

means current direct person-to-person response in the presence of the Life-Giving Father. Here the seminal ethic appears as this childlike whole-person response, rather than as a barren code for mechanical conformity.

The New Testament stresses the sabbatic dependence (and corporate interdependence) of persons by reinforcing the Hebrew Scriptures' view of the liberated people as God's children. As I just mentioned, a leading motif of Jesus in the earliest Gospel, Mark, is that it is simply in being like *little children* that you will have lasting place in God's reign.[8] The latest of the Gospels, John, has a similar leitmotif expressed in Jesus' response to Nicodemus in Chapter 3, where rather than childlikeness, our even earlier, fetal life is his key image: Our rebirth is singled out alongside birth as the most important fact of life. More than anything else, our birth was sheer gift, utterly beyond our own causation or control—even our proudest self-control. Yet believed as gifted freedom, both our birth and rebirth entail new, unique creation.[9]

For Christian faith memories of Jesus are normative for what may be expected in human terms of God's life-giving freedom. Should we be tempted to lay claim to contrary inspirations, as if the Holy Spirit would lead away from his grace, we venture onto rocky ground that is littered with the bloodied bones of old heresies.[10]

As fallible mortal creatures, then, *Spirit-gifted* healing or rebirth in wholeness is finally our life's key. "Who by taking thought can add a cubit to his own age" or inner stature? "Think how it is

---

8. See Mark 10:13-15. Note also the following negative case narrative example, where the rich man's question of "What can I do?" exhibits an opposite, non-childlike stance (Mark 10:17-37; see also 9:35-37).

9. Professor Charles Myers of Gettysburg College makes a provocative contribution to Reformed liturgy by introducing as a part of the confessional an exchange between worshippers: "You are accepted, you are forgiven; and there's nothing *you* can do about it !"

10. Numerous outrageous examples range from Jan van Leiden's (i.e., Johann Backelsohn's) New Jerusalem takeover of Muenster (1534) to Jim Jones' People's Temple with the poisoned Kool Aid sacramental deaths of 913 persons in his South American jungle commune (1978) along with many other ecstatic sects and end-of-world cults which have boasted of being uniquely Spirit-inspired.

that the lilies grow."[11] We do not heal ourselves by tugging at our own moral bootstraps any more than we can re-enter our "mother's womb a second time and be born." Being who we are, healing becomes a prime content of sabbatic relationship, as we depend on God in Christ, the healer, for life renewal—this at the initiative of the Holy Spirit, who like wind "spirits where he will."[12]

Some of the earliest symbolic graphic portrayals on first-century Christian tombs picture a youth in the Moses pose, striking the water of life from a rock. Sometimes this image is melded together with Jesus in the same Moses pose, raising Lazarus from a stone sepulcher, healing a sick child, or filling the water crocks with the wine of new life. Clearly, these symbolic meanings were seen to coalesce. For all resonate with the Exodus story's complete dependence of a people for liberation, the gift of abiding abundant life, and finally of our resurrection itself. As Ernst Käsemann sums it up, "the power of Jesus' Resurrection becomes a reality here and now in the form of Christian freedom, and only in that."[13] So our life's dominant mode and mood may be, and is to be, that of lighthearted comedy in the sense that "all's well that ends well."

## 4) Gratitude as Our Life Attitude

The Heidelberg Catechism is instructive in the way, through its very structure, it unfolds the nucleus of New Testament ethics. For it subsumes all it has to say about life-formation, law-keeping, community-building, and even church organization under the single rubric, *Von der Dankbarkeyt* (About Gratitude).[14] Grace-responsive gratitude motivates Christians' affects and shapes their actions. Our direct response to the gracious One, who, as faith discovers, has revealed himself in Christ and who is constantly present as the Spirit, is equally to be described as a *sabbatic ethic*. This

---

11. Mark 6:27-28; Luke 12:25-27. Surely this reflection includes what we might call one's moral stature.

12. John 3:3-8.

13. Käsemann, *Jesus Means Freedom*, 154.

14. Question 86 ff.

is an ethic of complete freedom in which all our self-expressions, non-verbal and verbal, gradually begin to *rest upon* his grace as our *grateful* response. As such all practical actions, in view of and responsive to, God's loving presence become concomitant with prayer, as our return of grace.[15]

## 5) Christians' Action as Prayer's Extension

This freedom is always within the relationship with God in his unswervingly gracious presence. All action has become conversational expression—always I-Thou in nature, as Martin Buber, the Jewish prophetic scholar, used to express it—always between you and your neighbor, and you both and your God. Hopefully, in Christ, God lets himself be known in the most intimate way for such relationship. In his continuing presence, all actions are matrixed in that relationship and hence—please note this key point—all actions effectively become *extensions of prayer*. Paul's "Pray without ceasing," is far more than pious advice to pray more often. If everything we are is open to God's loving presence, we begin to understand that our every move will have this communal concomitance with prayer—and as such, can have eternal significance.[16]

I am not saying that your conduct must appear to be piously prayerful; rather your most robust, practical, political effort or your most tender, private, or sexual interplay is to become a dimension of prayer—and prayer-dimensioned within our Sabbatic relationship. In line with this, the great seventeenth-century Puritan spokesman William Perkins (1602) used to say that all of life is to become a *continual Sabbath rest*. And for him that meant something joyful, quite unlike the later blue-stocking-Puritans' rigid and morose front-parlor Sabbath-keeping.

---

15. See Questions 116 and following with Eph 5:20 in mind: "always and for everything giving thanks."

16. For Paul, essential gratitude is expressed not only in actual prayers, but in "salty" conversation as well as in all other activities. See Col 4:2–6 (also as echoed in the Pauline Epistle of Eph 5:20).

If you like pasting on labels, you could well tag Christians' seminal way-of-life teaching *a sabbatic ethic of free, pneumatic response*. Companionship with the Holy Spirit here does not mean we piously become "more spiritual" (whatever that's supposed to mean!) and certainly not that we become somehow "spiritually" above any of our neighbors or detached from the mundane nitty-gritty, but quite the opposite: our most grungy tasks and sweaty sex, as well as our most playful flights of imagination, are to take on sanctity as part of our wholehearted, full-bodied converse with the One we've come to know in Christ, who we've been given to believe will be with us to the ends of the cosmos.

## 6) Play's the Thing—Refreshing Our Work Ethic

The theology of play should be of special concern. "Life should be play"—not constraint.[17] For it is of crucial importance in a post-industrial society, where automation, cybernetics, and artificial intelligence will continue to whittle away on the amount of labor actually needed for life support. Here Christians have a special political calling where they may act as leaven to enlighten our economy regarding the full worth of a light and playful enjoyment of each other as ends-in-self within grace. This is nothing frivolous, for we are called to be a catalyst toward dissolving the mercenary structures that have depersonalized working people into mere "human resources." Notice that this offers a real solution to the enormous social problems caused by the loss of industrial production jobs. It may be, as secular philosopher Bertrand Russell long ago observed, that there is far too much work being done. The Protestant work ethic needs to be grasped anew in terms of free play in grace.

Because play is so crucial in creaturely fulfillment, its devaluation or prostitution entails some of our most serious ethical problems. Distorted forms of play plague us: There is the sexual dalliance that puts the moment's orgasm above love's loyalty. There

---

17. Ellul, *To Will and to Do*, 60.

are the high-risk or brain-bruising sports that put adrenalin jag above simple appreciation of gifted play together. There is the "gaming," the gambling that can become a fatal addiction and put both family and career at risk. There are those arenas where competitive pride has turned sports into forms of warfare rather than mutual enjoyment. And ironically, as Huizinga[18] and others have long pointed out, military conflict—warfare itself—often becomes the most grievously bastardized and evil form of play. Again, because in the light of the New Testament good play is so crucial in human fulfillment, its distorted forms become most pressing ethical problems.

In the I-Thou intercourse of responsive relationships, Christians will leaven the workplace and yet give weight even to chance meetings, delighting in the full worth of playful encounter—enjoying each other as ends-in-self within grace without turning people into mere "human resources" or cogs in a machine for production or economic gain. As we realize the full worth of playful encounters, the entire economy shifts and no longer has its primary energies invested in the production of material "goods." Not only are traditional "services" and "helping professions" enhanced and elevated in their relative economic worth, but also are a myriad of other activities wherein people enjoy each other for their own sakes or simply are absorbed in the exploration of the boundless givenness surrounding us—all in a playful fascination and gratitude for the world of nature. Endless vocations are engendered where our faith gives the fullest value to such adult and sophisticated forms of play, quite apart from necessary industrial production. (Of course, even welding and bolt-tightening could be infused with the spirit of play for challenging labor does not have to be slavish or mind-numbing.)

But think here of the arts, literature, theatre, the exploration of nature, festive celebration, travel, hostelry, sports, games, liturgics, and worship. All these may in effect become vital forms of play in which our human intercourse is valued as end-in-itself—a joyous exploration or celebration, either of each others' God-given

18. See Johan Huizinga's *Homo Ludens* (1949).

ETHICS STRIPPED DOWN FOR THE WORLD

intelligence and skills[19] or of the profound ecology in which we find ourselves embedded.

My most immediate example from my time of retirement is the rewarding fascination I am finding at the keyboard. Despite a rather mediocre musical talent, as I explore even the simplest chordal and rhythmic combinations, this very narrow slice of the vast gift of Creation (sound waves with their frequencies grasped as just twelve tones) offers virtually unending creative potential. In the *playing and interplaying* of music, this narrow band of God's creation can be explored in almost endless variety. It is astounding how further play just here provides a full vocation and livelihood for countless composers, instrumentalists, and jazz improvisers. The same sort of observation can be made regarding the potential playful engagement offered by hundreds of other slices of the givenness of Nature. When the Creation is valued as a superabundant, feast-like gift of grace, we find ourselves endowed with material for endless exploration and creative extemporization. Our calling to such free play in grace is to be enjoyed and treasured in any of thousands of fields.

Of course to be truly gracious and playful, such activities would have to engender Christ-like freedom. In professional sport, film, literature, and research we find ourselves all too often galled by money-grubbing, hero worship, competitive hubris, and other forms of idolatry that can corrupt such activities or hobble them with incongruous forms of compulsion. The news every day exposes such moral problems in professional sport organizations, film corporations, research institutions, etc. Because of the importance of such areas for liberated and liberating community, such parodies of play present social-ethical problems of the heaviest order.

We give high moral order to questions of sexual conduct, not because we think sex is unimportant or something to be suppressed

---

19. Col 4:6; Mark 9:50; Matt 5:13; Luke 14:34. In this connection, a fresh exploration of the closely related dynamic of improvisation in Christians' lives is offered by Anglican Vicar Samuel Wells in his book *Improvisation: The Drama of Christian Ethics*.

and ignored, but because as one of God's grand ideas, sexual interplay is a blessing to be tendered and protected from abuse. In analogy, we will give serious attention to political abuses, where activities and vocations which could express the play of grace are dragged into compulsive or competitive parodies of true community or where one or another meritocracy is allowed to poison it.

But despite the moral ambiguities that emerge here (as everywhere in human affairs), there are countless paying jobs to be generated around these kinds of supra-industrial activities. As Christians promote the ultimate importance of sheer play, expansion here will more than compensate for job losses of the industrial type—many of them onerous, sweaty, mechanical, and mind-numbing—where workers are being displaced by automation and cybernetics. So, strange as it may seem, our socioeconomic worries really have to do with a lack of faith and can find their solution right there. Relief from the industrial age's compulsive slavery to the production of material stuff should be a blessing.

All in all, we have found the New Testament's micro-ethic phenomenon was no accident. Christians' ethic from the very beginning has been communicated *in nuce*. Our lives do unfold and blossom from a seed-like experience of grace. We are given to believe that it is by God's further initiative *in Christ* that they are faith-fructified and given everlasting substance. It is in spontaneous conversational response that we begin to experience such "fruit of the Spirit": original creative community-building action in a playful freedom that is expressive of gratitude and radiant joy—spreading light, levity, and salty wit.

# ABSTRACT

My summary, then, is this: If we re-examine our apostolic origins, we observe how, from their earliest beginnings, Christians' way of life has always unfolded quite spontaneously from a simple, seminal grace claim, a *kerygmatic micro-ethic*. To grasp the nature of Christians' life, it is crucial to observe how it has all unfolded and continues to unfold from this small genetic germ in faith's dawning awareness of God's grace. What unfolds is an attitude of free, even playful, direct engagement and response.

The first believers focused enthusiastically on the living Christ. Enjoying a radically *christocentric* way of life, they believed they were called to follow the risen Lord into ever-new surroundings. Therefore we'd do well to characterize their responsive action as freely following the living Person, the Holy Spirit, who is first known in human terms through Jesus Christ. (So call it also a *pneumatic ethic* if you will.) It finds itself freely engaged by a living Lord, with far more fluidity than a rigid imitation of Jesus. (So we would have to regard the church's emerging christocentric way of life as more christo*tropic* than cristo*morphic*—always creatively *following*, rather than passively conforming.) This means we should always think in terms of the *active life of Christians* and avoid presuming to abstract and prescribe a rigid "*Christian way of life*."

Since Jesus was believed to fulfill and extend the ancient faith, focused in the Mosaic liberation events, we have observed how Christians' faith-impregnated lifestyle is also a *sabbatic ethic*, a matter of pledged interdependence in God's liberty-bound community.

Spontaneous and wholehearted, it is to be quite shamelessly free. Jesus Christ, the healer, is our sole final judge, representing one who will restore us and leave all alienation and brokenness behind. The New Testament's seminal ethic, as it unfolds for us, is therefore finally a *comedic ethic*. (For "all's well that ends well!")

Since our Christian life is always rediscovered as our mutual interdependence within God's Christ-borne love, it is to be experienced as community "in Christ," so it is always a *covenantal, corporate,* and *conversational* ethic. In the supple life here taking form, we find the stuff of human fulfillment and joy.

# BIBLIOGRAPHY

Anderson, Raymond Kemp. *An American Scholar Recalls Karl Barth's Golden Years As a Teacher, 1958-1964: The Mature Theologian.* Lewiston, NY: Mellen, 2013.
———. "Corporate Selfhood and *Meditatio Vitae Futura*: How Necessary Is Eschatology for Christian Ethics?" *Journal of the Society of Christian Ethics* 23.1 (2003) 21-46.
———. *Karl Barth's Table Talk . . . 1958-1964.* Lewiston, NY: Mellen, 2014.
———. *Liberating Speech—Today: Essays on the Freedom to Speak Out (or Hold Your Tongue) in an Interconnected World.* Eugene, OR: Wipf and Stock, 2015.
———. "Love and Order: The Life Structuring Dynamics of Grace and Virtue in Calvin's Ethical Thought: An Interpretation." PhD diss., University of Basel, 1973.
———. *On Trusting Freedom: The First Christians' Genotype for Multicultural Living.* Eugene, OR: Resource, 2018.
Baker, Wesley C. *The Open End of Christian Morals.* Philadelphia: Westminster, 1967.
Barth, Karl. *Die kirchliche Dogmatik.* 4 vols. Zollikon-Zürich: Evangelischer Verlag, 1936-1968.
———. *Eklärung des Philipperbriefes.* Zollikon-Zürich: Evangelischer Verlag, 1947.
———. "The Word of God and the Task of Ministry." In *The Word of God and the Word of Man*, translated by Douglas Horton, 183-217. London, Hodder & Stoughton, 1928.
Branscomb, B. Harvie. *The Message of Jesus.* Nashville: Cokesbury, 1926.
Brunner, Emil. *The Divine Imperative.* Philadelphia: Westminster, 1947.
———. *The Divine-Human Encounter.* London: SCM, 1944.
Bultmann, Rudolf. *Jesus and the Word.* New York: Scribners, 1958.
———. "The Primitive Christian Kerygma and the Historical Jesus." In *The Historical Jesus and the Kerygmatic Christ*, edited by Carl E. Braaten and Roy A. Harrisville, 15-42. Nashville: Abingdon, 1964.

## BIBLIOGRAPHY

———. *Primitive Christianity in its Contemporary Sources*. Cleveland: World, 1956.
———. *Theology of the New Testament*. New York: Scribner, 1951.
Cone, James H. *The Spirituals and the Blues*. Maryknoll: Orbis, 1972.
Cullmann, Oscar. *Christ and Time: The Primitive Christian Conception of Time and History*. Translated by Floyd V. Filson. Philadelphia: Westminster, 1950.
———. *Études de Theologie Biblique*. Neuchâtel: Delachaux et Niestlé, 1968.
———. "Immortality of the Soul, or Resurrection of the Dead: The Witness of the New Testament." In *Immortality and Resurrection: Death in the Western World: Two Conflicting Currents of Thought*, edited by Krister Stendahl, 9–53. New York: Macmillan, 1965.
Dodd, C. H. *The Apostolic Teaching and its Developments*. London: Hodder & Stoughton, 1936.
Ellul, Jacques. *To Will and to Do: An Ethical Research for Christians*. Philadelphia: Pilgrim, 1969.
Fletcher, Joseph. *Moral Responsibility: Situation Ethics at Work*. London: SCM, 1967.
———. *Situation Ethic: The New Morality*. Philadelphia: Westminster, 1966.
Grayston, Kenneth. *The Letters of Paul to the Philippians and to the Thessalonians*. The Cambridge Bible Commentary on the New English Bible. Cambridge: Cambridge University Press, 1967.
Hauerwas, Stanley M. *Christian Existence Today*. Grand Rapids: Baker, 1988.
Hauerwas, Stanley M., et al. *Truthfulness and Tragedy: Further Investigations into Christian Ethics*. Notre Dame: University of Notre Dame Press, 1977.
Herzog, Frederick. *Liberation Theology: Liberation in the Light of the Fourth Gospel*. New York: Seabury, 1972.
Houlden, J. L. *Ethics and the New Testament*. London: T. & T. Clark, 1973.
Huizinga, Johan. *Homo Ludens*. London: Routledge and Kegan, 1949.
Hunter, Archibald. *The Message of the New Testament*. Philadelphia: Westminster, 1953.
Kant, Immanuel. *Fundamental Principles of the Metaphysics of Ethics*. London: Longmans, Green & Co., 1946.
Käsemann, Ernst. *Jesus Means Freedom*. London: SCM, 1969.
Kümmel, Werner G. *The New Testament: The History of the Investigation of its Problems*. Nashville: Abingdon, 1972.
Leeuw, Gerardus van der. *Sacred and Profane Beauty: The Holy in Art*. London: Holt, Rinehart and Winston, 1963.
Lehmann, Paul, *Ethics in a Christian Context*. New York: Harper & Row, 1963.
Løgstrup, Knud E. *The Ethical Demand*. Philadelphia: Fortress, 1971.
Lohse, Eduard. *Theological Ethics of the New Testament*. Minneapolis: Fortress, 1991.
Manson, T. W. *The Teaching of Jesus: Studies of Form and Content*. London: Cambridge University Press, 1963.

# BIBLIOGRAPHY

Marshall, L. H. *The Challenge of New Testament Ethics*. London: Macmillan, 1948.

Moffic, Evan. *The Way of Jesus Christ*. Minneapolis: Fortress, 1993.

———. *What Every Christian Needs to Know About the Jewishness of Jesus*. Nashville: Abingdon, 2015.

Moltmann. Jürgen. *Ethics of Hope*. Minneapolis: Fortress, 2012.

———. "The Messianic Sabbath." In *The Way of Jesus Christ*, 199–21. Minneapolis: Fortress, 1995.

———. *The Way of Jesus Christ*. Minneapolis: Fortress, 1995.

Niebuhr, Reinhold. *An Interpretation of Christian Ethics*. New York: Harper, 1935.

Outka, Gene H. *Agape—An Ethical Analysis*. New Haven: Yale University Press, 1972.

Reumann, John. *Jesus in the Church's Gospels: Modern Scholarship and the Earliest Sources*. Philadelphia: Fortress, 1968.

Richardson, Alan. *The Political Christ*. Philadelphia: Westminster, 1973.

Richardson, Peter. *Paul's Ethic of Freedom*. Philadelphia: Westminster, 1979.

Robinson, John A. T. *Honest to God*. London: SCM, 1963.

———. "Law and Love." In *On Being Responsible: Issues in Personal Ethics*, edited by James M. Gustafson and James T. Laney, 184–97. New York: Harper and Row, 1968.

———. *On Being the Church in the World*. Philadelphia: Westminster, 1960.

Russell, Bertrand. *A History of Western Philosophy*. London: Allen and Unwin, 1945.

Sanders, Jack T. *Ethics in the New Testament*. Philadelphia: Fortress, 1975.

Schubert, Kurt. *Die Religion des nachbiblischen Judentums*. Freiburg: Herder, 1973.

Scott, Ernest F., and Robert R. Wicks. "The Epistle to the Philippians." In *The Interpreter's* Bible, edited by George A. Buttrick, 11:3–129. New York: Abingdon, 1955.

Sigal, Phillip. *The Emergence of Contemporary Judaism*. Vol. 1, *The Foundations of Judaism from Biblical Origins to the Sixth Century A.D. Part 1, From the Origins to the Separation of Christianity*. Edited by Dikran Hadidian. PTMS 29. Pittsburgh: Pickwick, 1980.

Sittler, Joseph. *The Structure of Christian Ethics*. Louisville: Westminster John Knox, 1958.

Thurneysen, Eduard. *Der Brief des Paulus an die Philipper ausgelegt für die Gemeinde*. Basel: Reinhardt, c. 1943.

———. *The Sermon on the Mount*. Richmond, VA: John Knox, 1964.

Verhey, Allen. *The Great Reversal: Ethics and the New Testament*. Grand Rapids: Eerdmans, 1986.

Wells, Samuel. *Improvisation: The Drama of Christian Ethics*. Grand Rapids: Baker, 2004.

## BIBLIOGRAPHY

Wendland, Heinz Dietrich. *Ethik des Neuen Testaments: Eine Einführung*. 2nd ed. Grundrisse zum Neuen Testament 4. Göttingen: Vandenhoeck and Ruprecht, 1975.

Wright, N. T. *The Day the Revolution Began: Reconsidering the Meaning of Jesus' Crucifixion*. New York: HarperCollins, 2016.

———. *Paul and the Faithfulness of God: Books I and II*. Christian Origins and the Question of God 4. Minneapolis: Fortress, 2013.

———. *Surprised by Hope: Rethinking Heaven, the Resurrection, and the Mission of the Church*. New York: HarperCollins, 2008.

# INDEX

actions
  *actions de grace*, 53–54
  actions vs. words? 37
  concomitant with prayer, 86
adoption, 52–53, 56
affection, 31, 35, 43, 53
Augustine, 23, 38
automation, 87, 90

Barth, Karl, 24, 38, 42, 50, 67–68
Baur, F. C., 6, 16
Brunner, Emil, 7, 26
Buber, Martin, 86
Bultmann, Rudolf, 3–4, 7, 18

Calvin, John, 9, 32–33, 42, 52, 54, 56, 60, 75, 82–83
*chesed* or *agape*, 11, 35–36, 43
Christocentrism, 45, 91
Christology, 57
church and state, 38
coercion, 38, 41
community, 42
compulsion, 12, 34, 40
corporate life, 39, 42, 44, 51, 75, 92
  as humanity, 39
  interdependence, 39, 83–84
  wholeness, 19–20, 26, 84
Council of Trent, 55–56
covenant renewal, 20–21, 41, 92
creativity, 24, 28, 57, 63, 78

cross-cultural flexibility, 80
Cullmann, Oscar, 18–19

disciplines and freedom, 29
diversity, 24, 57, 81
dualism, 20, 33
  Hellenistic, 18, 20
  modern, 18, 21
duty, 12–13, 15, 32, 34

economics, 88
election, 18, 52
enjoyment, 59, 80, 88
Ellul, Jacques, 87
Erasmus, 16, 33
Eschatology, 6, 17–18, 21
  Judaic, 17–21
ethics
  as fun, 81
  Christian ethic, a misnomer? 31
  Christomorphic and Christotropic, 91
  conversational, 92
  flexible, 23, 30, 45, 47, 61, 63, 67, 76–77, 80
  of direct response, 15, 24–25, 62, 85
  of imagination, x, 27, 80, 87
  of pneumatic response, 25, 81, 87, 91
  play, x, 87–89
  sabbatic ethics, 83–84

# INDEX

ethics *(continued)*
  seminal, 76–79, 81
  situation ethic, 8, 62, 82
  extemporization, 89

faith
  faith's apperception, 31, 53
  *fides informata / formata*, 56
  justified *by* faith? 52
Fletcher, Joseph, 31, 34–35, 62
frame of reference, 39, 57
freedom, 30, 47–49, 73
  as obedience, 46
  radical, 63
  trust in, 10, 24, 45, 79–82
free response, 10, 67, 73, 78
free will, 16, 33–34

gambling, 88
*gnosis*, 18, 48
God
  freedom of, 57
  healing intent, 7
  presence of, 66
  veiled and unknown, 12, 16–17, 38, 55, 75
golden rule, 64, 77
government, 37–38, 40, 73
  covenanted freedom, 73
grace, 8, 24
  ethical imperative, 52
  life's matrix, 51
  motivating gratitude, 52, 54–55, 85
  non-categorization, 36, 74
  priority of, 50
  redefines justice, 11
  upwards spiral of, 35, 50
grace-responsive life, 50, 54
greatness, 38, 56–57

*halakah*, 5, 40
Harnack, Adolph von, 6
Hauerwas, Stanley, 11, 59–60, 68
Heidelberg Catechism, 54, 85

Hellenistic
  cults, 48
  cultural confrontation, 48–49
Hillel, Rabbi, 77
Holy Spirit, 51, 55, 66, 76, 84
  initiative of, 85
Houlden, J. L., 10, 48, 59, 73, 75
Huizinga, Johan, 88
human resources, 26, 87–88

identity, 52, 54
immortality? 19
inspiration, 26, 84
interim ethic? 18, 21
*I-Thou*, 86, 88

Jeremiah, 10, 15
Jesus Christ
  apocalyptic of, 17–18
  childlikeness as norm, 83
  end of law, 42
  eschatology of, 6, 17–21
  great reversal, 72, 75
  imitation of 28, 43, 72
  "liberal" view of, 6, 17
  life in Christ, 15, 38, 57, 59, 60, 92
  living norm, 25, 38–42, 84
  moral pioneer? 6–7, 16–17
  revealer, 3, 7, 13, 85
  role, 4
  sole judge, 42
  symbolic portrayal of, 42, 44, 85
job creation, 87–88, 90
joy, 60, 72, 86
justification, 50–55
  God's sovereign act, 51
  *simul iustus et peccator*, 36

Kant, Immanuel, 31, 34
*karma*, 33
Käsemann, Ernst, 85
*kerygma*, 24
Kierkegaard, Søren, 17, 83
King, Martin Luther, Jr., 37

# INDEX

Kümmel, Werner, 6

labor, 88
law, 30
  as love, 25, 43, 77
  canon law, 9, 24, 56, 68, 73–74, 80
  civil laws, 37, 73
  natural law? 74–75
  sacred, 43
  Torah, 40–44
Lohse, Eduard, 5, 64
love, 52
  *agape / chesed*, 11, 35–36, 43
  command, 36, 77
  excruciating demand, 34
  gifted, 36
  impossible inperative, 8
  opportunistic, 27
  spontaneous, 34
Love! as law kills, 35–36
Luther, Martin, 16, 32–33, 83

Macmurray, John, 12
Manson, T.W., 5
Marcion, 83
Mead. George F., 37
*metanoio*, 24, 62, 82
missionary concern, 63, 67–68
Moffic, Evan, 76
Moltmann, Jürgen, 9, 18, 21, 59
motivation, gratitude, 85
Myers, Charles, 84

nativism, 39
natural law, 74–75

obedience, 16, 31, 46, 54, 72, 81–82

Paul
  and Law, 40–42, 63
  background & role, 48, 65
  difficult? 46
  liberation doctrine, 49

  opponents, 45- 46
  reception-response order, 50
  scandal of, 45
  transcultural freedom, 23, 61–63
  urging (paraenesis), 23, 48
  virtue catalogues? 46, 59, 61, 69
Pentecost, 55, 65–66
Perkins, William, 86
person response, 2, 77, 80
Pharisaic Christians, 45, 63
play, 87–89
  corruption of, 87
  jazz improvization, 89
  sexual, 87, 89
  valuation of, 88
playful encounter, 88
political action, 39–40, 73
prayer, 30
  as faith's inception, 54–55
  concomitant with action (*praxis*), 86
principles, 77–78

repentance / reorientation, 24, 49, 62, 82
resurrection, 7, 66, 85
  bodily, 19, 22
  holistic, 21
  promise, 41
Ritschl, Albrecht, 6
Robinson, John A.T., 5, 31, 62
Russell, Bertrand, 87

Sabbath, 2, 76–77
  Sabbath-keeping, 86
sabbatic ethic, 20, 80, 87, 91
sabbatic life, x, 20–21, 41, 76, 84
sacrament, 26, 38, 42
sacrifice, 66
  of Isaac, 83
salt and leaven, 28
sanctification, 53–54
  as God's sovereign act, 51–53, 55

# INDEX

Shammai, Rabbi, 77
simultaneity, 20
*Situation Ethics*, 31–32, 34, 62
slavery, 29, 40, 47, 74
*sola fidei*, 52, 82,
*sola scriptura*, 1
Spirit-response vs. "spirituality," 13, 25, 33, 83
spontaneity, 15, 72, 75, 90–92
*syllogismus practicus*, 56

Thurneysen, Eduard, 9, 61

Time-Space, 19–21, 47

unity in diversity, 25–26

Verhey, Allen, 69, 75
virtue, 11, 31, 59–60, 67, 75

Weiss, Johannes, 17, 20
work ethic, 87–88
Wright, N. T., 19–21, 68, 73

Yoder, John Howard, 11

www.ingramcontent.com/pod-product-compliance
Lightning Source LLC
Chambersburg PA
CBHW070930160426
43193CB00011B/1634